It's another great book from CGP...

Quite a bit of maths crops up when you're studying science,
so you need to know how to handle it when it does.

But don't panic. This book covers the maths that you're likely to meet,
with plenty of worked examples and practice questions.

There are questions relating to Biology, Chemistry and Physics
— so we've got it all covered.

CGP — still the best! ☺

Our sole aim here at CGP is to produce the highest quality books —
carefully written, immaculately presented and dangerously close to being funny.

Then we work our socks off to get them out to you
— at the cheapest possible prices.

Published by CGP

Editors:
Katherine Craig, Rachel Kordan, Sarah Pattison.

ISBN: 978 1 84762 469 7

With thanks to Glenn Rogers and Jamie Sinclair for the proofreading.

Clipart from Corel®
Printed by Elanders Ltd, Newcastle upon Tyne

Based on the classic CGP style created by Richard Parsons.

Text, design, layout and original illustrations © Coordination Group Publications Ltd. (CGP) 2013
All rights reserved.

Photocopying more than one chapter of this book is not permitted. Extra copies are available from CGP.
0800 1712 712 • www.cgpbooks.co.uk

Contents

Section 1 — Calculations
Calculating the Mean and Range 2
Calculating Percentages 4
Substituting Values into Formulas 6
Rearranging Formulas 8

Section 2 — Presenting Data
Drawing Tables 10
Drawing Bar Charts 12
Drawing Line Graphs 16
Drawing Scatter Graphs 20
Drawing Pie Charts 24
Drawing Histograms 28

Section 3 — Analysing Data
Interpreting Tables 32
Interpreting Bar Charts 34
Interpreting Line Graphs 38
Interpreting Scatter Graphs 42
Interpreting Pie Charts 46
Interpreting Histograms 48
Distance-Time Graphs — Calculating Speed 50
Velocity-Time Graphs — Calculating Acceleration 52
Velocity-Time Graphs — Calculating Distance 54
Conclusions and Evaluations 56

Glossary 61
Index 62

Section 1 — Calculations

Calculating the Mean and Range

The mean result isn't just a nasty bit of data that won't share its chips — it's the average of the results from the various repeats of an experiment. Meanwhile, the range is a value that tells you how spread out your data is. They both come in useful when you've got some results to analyse, so here's how you work them out.

Example

Some students were investigating the effect of temperature on the time taken for a reaction to finish.

Their results are shown in the table on the right.

a) Calculate the mean time for each temperature.
b) Calculate the range of times for the three temperatures.

Temperature (°C)	Repeats (s)		
	1	2	3
10	56	57	55
20	41	44	42
30	32	30	43

1 To find a mean, you need to add together the results and then divide by the total number of results.

Temperature (°C)	Repeats (s)			Mean (s)
	1	2	3	
10	56	57	55	$\frac{56 + 57 + 55}{3} = 56$
20	41	44	42	$\frac{41 + 44 + 42}{3} = 42.333... = 42$
30	32	30	43	$\frac{32 + 30}{2} = 31$

First, add together the results for the 3 repeats.

There are 3 results for 10 °C so you divide by 3.

You're only using 2 results here so you just need to divide by 2.

Sometimes you get a result that doesn't fit in with the rest of the repeats. These are called anomalous results. You don't include them when you're calculating the mean. Here, 43 is an anomalous result because it's much higher than 32 and 30.

2 Give the answer to a sensible number of significant figures.

- The first significant figure is the first digit in a number which isn't a zero. The digits after that are numbered the 2nd, 3rd, 4th, etc. significant figures.

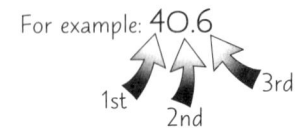

For example: 40.6
1st 2nd 3rd

- Sometimes the question will tell you how many significant figures to use. If not, you should just use your common sense to round to a similar length to the other data in the question.

- All you need to do is look to the next digit to the right. If it's 5 or more, round up. If it's 4 or less, round down.

- The mean result for the experiment at 20 °C is 42.333... s. This rounds down to 42 s to 2 significant figures (s.f.).

42.333 → 42 to 2 significant figures

We want to round to 2 significant figures, so look at the third significant figure. It's 4 or less, so round down.

3 To find the range for the data, subtract the smallest number from the biggest number.

Temperature (°C)	Repeats (s)			Range (s)
	1	2	3	
10	56	57	55	57 − 55 = 2
20	41	44	42	44 − 41 = 3
30	32	30	43	32 − 30 = 2

43 is an anomalous result, so don't include it in the calculation.

Calculating the Mean and Range

Now you get a chance to practise all that. After all, it would be mean of me not to give you any questions...

Q1 John carried out an experiment to measure the resistance of two different lengths of wire. His results are below. Calculate the mean resistance and range for each wire. **PHYSICS**

Wire	Repeat 1 (Ω)	Repeat 2 (Ω)	Repeat 3 (Ω)
1	5	4	6
2	9	10	8

Q2 Nadia is testing reflex reactions by timing how long it takes each person to respond to a tap on their leg. She repeats the experiment three times. Calculate the mean and range of her results for each person. **BIOLOGY**

Person	Reaction time (s)		
	Repeat 1	Repeat 2	Repeat 3
A	0.04	0.05	0.04
B	0.07	0.06	0.05
C	0.05	0.04	0.03
D	0.30	0.05	0.05

Q3 Some students investigated the energy content of 3 different fuels. Calculate the mean energy content and the range for each fuel. **CHEMISTRY**

Fuel	Energy (J/g)				
	Repeat 1	Repeat 2	Repeat 3	Repeat 4	Repeat 5
A	28.2	30.9	33.1	31.2	30.5
B	16.7	15.5	6.1	18.3	16.1
C	10.2	9.8	11.6	8.7	10.9

Section 1 — Calculations

Calculating Percentages

Percentages are 100% useful. You could be asked to work one out from some data, so it's a good idea to know how to do it. It's really not that tricky though, once you know what you're doing.

Example

Dave collected some data about the blood types of students in his class. His results are in the table opposite.

Blood type	A	B	AB	O
Number of students	20	6	1	23

What percentage of the students have blood type O?

1 Add together all of the results.

Blood type	A	B	AB	O
Number of students	20	6	1	23

$20 + 6 + 1 + 23 = 50$

So there are 50 students in total.

2 Read off the value of the category in the question, and divide it by the total of the results.

Blood type	A	B	AB	O
Number of students	20	6	1	23

The question asks about blood type O. The table shows that 23 students have this blood type, so divide this by the total number of students:

$23 \div 50 = 0.46$

3 Multiply that number by 100 to get the percentage.

$0.46 \times 100 = 46\%$

So 46% of the students have blood type O.

Example

The table on the right shows how much gas is produced during a reaction at 10-second intervals.

Time (s)	0	10	20	30	40	50
Amount of gas (cm³)	0	36	45	54	60	64

What is the percentage change in the amount of gas produced between 10 s and 30 s?

1 Work out the difference between the two amounts by subtracting the smaller amount from the larger amount.

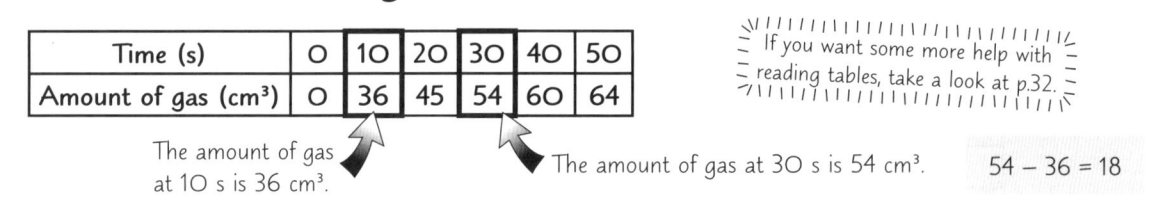

Time (s)	0	10	20	30	40	50
Amount of gas (cm³)	0	36	45	54	60	64

The amount of gas at 10 s is 36 cm³. The amount of gas at 30 s is 54 cm³. $54 - 36 = 18$

If you want some more help with reading tables, take a look at p.32.

2 Then use this equation: $\text{percentage change} = \dfrac{\text{difference}}{\text{starting amount}} \times 100$

The difference between the two amounts of gas is 18 cm³. The earlier amount of gas is 36 cm³.

$\dfrac{18}{36} \times 100 = 50\%$

So the percentage change between 10 s and 30 s is 50%.

Section 1 — Calculations

Calculating Percentages

Back to you now. Grab a calculator and have a go at these questions...

Q1 Mike recorded the masses of different food groups in one type of food. His results are shown in the table below. What percentage of the food is protein? **BIOLOGY**

Food group	Mass (g)
Carbohydrate	10
Protein	9
Fat	5
Other	6

Q2 The table below shows the mass of product formed in a reaction after certain time intervals. Work out the percentage change in the mass of product made between 10 and 20 s. **CHEMISTRY**

Time (s)	0	10	20	30
Mass (g)	0	6	10	13

Q3 The table below shows the change in the radioactivity of a substance over time. What is the percentage change in radioactivity between 1 and 2 hours? **PHYSICS**

Time (hours)	0	1	2	3	4
Activity (Bq)	850	212	55	12	3

Section 1 — Calculations

Substituting Values into Formulas

If you can use one formula you can use them all. They can look a bit daunting at first — but once you substitute the letters or words for numbers, you're usually just a simple calculation away from the answer.

Example

The table on the right shows the results of a bike race. Work out the distance that Jenny cycled.

	Speed (m/s)	Time (min)
Jenny	5	3
Max	7	2

1 Decide which formula you need to use.

You know the speed and the time taken. You want to find out the distance Jenny travelled. So you need a formula that includes those three things.

The one you need here is: **distance (m) = speed (m/s) × time (s)**

Depending on what course you're doing, you'll either have to remember a bunch of formulas or they'll be given to you in the exam.

2 Substitute the numbers from the question into the formula.

distance = speed (m/s) × time (s)

Speed = 5 m/s

Time = 3 minutes
     = 3 × 60 = 180 seconds

So, distance = 5 m/s × 180 s

Make sure the numbers you're using are in the right units.

You need the time in seconds but you're given it in minutes in the table — you need to change it before you can put it in the formula.

3 Calculate the answer.

5 m/s × 180 s = **900 m**

Don't forget to include the units in your answer.

4 Take time to relax with some baking.

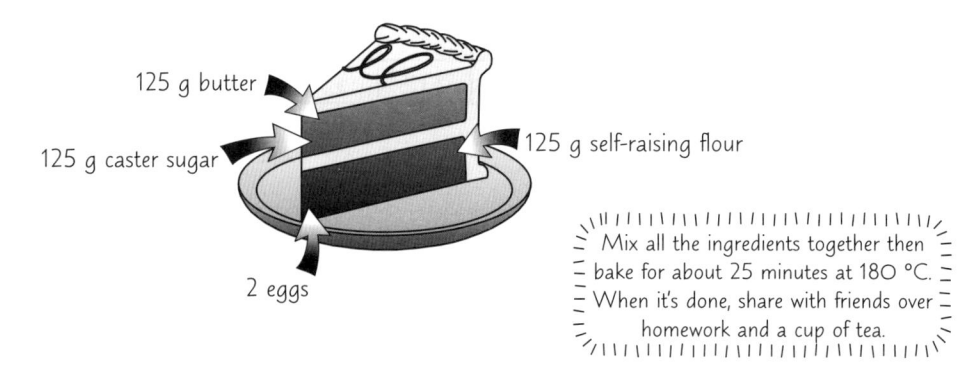

125 g butter

125 g caster sugar

125 g self-raising flour

2 eggs

Mix all the ingredients together then bake for about 25 minutes at 180 °C. When it's done, share with friends over homework and a cup of tea.

Section 1 — Calculations

Substituting Values into Formulas

Now it's time for you to plug some numbers into these formulas. Keep an eye on those pesky units...

Q1 Beth is 1.5 metres tall and has a body mass of 50 kg. What is her BMI?   **BIOLOGY**

$$BMI = \frac{Body\ mass\ (kg)}{(Height\ (m))^2}$$

Q2 A motor transfers 4.8 kJ of useful energy in 2 minutes. What is its power output?   **PHYSICS**

$$Power\ (W) = \frac{Work\ done\ (J)}{Time\ taken\ (s)}$$

1 kJ = 1000 J

Q3 Jared added 25 cm³ of sodium hydroxide solution to completely neutralise an acid during a titration. He calculated that this volume contained 0.0025 moles of sodium hydroxide. What was the concentration of the sodium hydroxide solution?   **CHEMISTRY**

$$Concentration\ (mol/dm^3) = \frac{Number\ of\ moles}{Volume\ (dm^3)}$$

1 dm³ = 1000 cm³

Q4 This table shows the force used to move two toy cars. Calculate the work done in moving each car.   **PHYSICS**

Car	Force (N)	Distance (cm)
A	5	157
B	10	223

Work done (J) = Force (N) × Distance (m)

Section 1 — Calculations

Rearranging Formulas

Formulas are generally straightforward, but sometimes you have to rearrange them before they're of any use. Don't panic though — there are just a few simple steps to follow to get everything swapped about.

Example A car is travelling at 6 m/s.
It accelerates at a rate of 1.54 m/s² for 2.6 seconds.
What is its final velocity?

1 Decide which formula you need to use.

You know the acceleration, the time and the car's initial velocity. You want to find out its final velocity. So you need to find a formula that includes those four things.

The one you want here is: $a = \dfrac{v - u}{t}$ — a stands for acceleration, v stands for final velocity, u stands for initial velocity, and t stands for time.

2 Decide what you need to make the subject.

$$a = \dfrac{v - u}{t}$$

You need to find out the final velocity so you need to get v on its own.

3 Rearrange the formula. You should always do the same thing to each side. To get rid of something you need to do the opposite. Keep going until you have the thing you want on its own.

$$a = \dfrac{v - u}{t}$$

The opposite of ÷t is ×t, so multiply both sides by t.

(× t) $a \times t = \dfrac{v - u}{t} \times t$

$a \times t = v - u$

The opposite of −u is +u, so add u to both sides.

(+ u) $(a \times t) + u = v - u + u$

$(a \times t) + u = v$

$v = (a \times t) + u$

Switch the sides round so that v is at the front.

The opposite of + is − and the opposite of − is +. The opposite of × is ÷ and the opposite of ÷ is ×.

4 Now you can just substitute the numbers in, and calculate the answer.

The acceleration (a) is 1.54 m/s².
Time (t) is 2.6 s.
The initial velocity (u) is 6 m/s.

$v = (a \times t) + u$
$v = (1.54 \times 2.6) + 6$
$v = \underline{10 \text{ m/s}}$ (2 s.f.)

5 Stroke a dog.

Maybe not this one.

Section 1 — Calculations

Rearranging Formulas

Right, your go. These formulas need a good swap about before you can answer the questions.

Q1 What is the mass of 4.2 moles of carbon (A_r = 12)?   **CHEMISTRY**

$$\text{Number of moles} = \frac{\text{Mass (g)}}{A_r}$$

Q2 A lamp is connected to a 2 V battery. The power of the lamp is 0.8 W. Calculate the current flowing through the lamp.   **PHYSICS**

$$\text{Power (W)} = \text{Current (A)} \times \text{Voltage (V)}$$

Q3 A radio wave in a vacuum has a frequency of 95.4×10^6 Hz. The speed of all electromagnetic waves in a vacuum is 3×10^8 m/s. Calculate the wavelength of the radio wave.   **PHYSICS**

$$\text{Speed (m/s)} = \text{Frequency (Hz)} \times \text{Wavelength (m)}$$

Q4 Phil has a BMI of 21.6. He has a body mass of 57 000 g. How tall is he?   **BIOLOGY**

$$\text{BMI} = \frac{\text{Body mass (kg)}}{(\text{Height (m)})^2}$$

TIP: The opposite of squaring something (^{2}) is to square root it ($\sqrt{}$).

Section 1 — Calculations

Section 2 — Presenting Data
Drawing Tables

Once you've collected some data, it's not much use unless it's organised in some way. Tables are a great way of doing this. When you've drawn a table you might then be able to spot patterns you never dreamed of... or at least it will make drawing a chart or graph easier.

Example

Below are the results of three repeats of an experiment in which the volume of gas produced in a reaction was measured at three temperatures, 10 °C, 20 °C and 30 °C. Put this data into a table.

10 °C	20 °C	30 °C		10 °C	20 °C	30 °C		10 °C	20 °C	30 °C
32 cm^3	60 cm^3	70 cm^3		28 cm^3	47 cm^3	68 cm^3		37 cm^3	51 cm^3	72 cm^3

1 Decide how many rows and columns you need.

Three temperatures were tested, so you need three rows plus a row or two for the headings.
The experiment was repeated three times, so you need four columns to include one for a heading.

2 Draw a nice, neat table using a ruler.

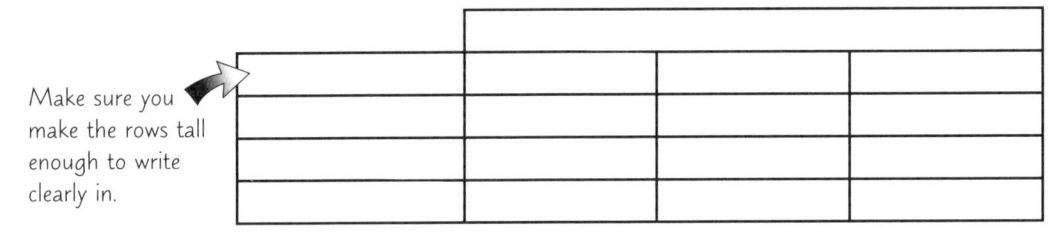

Make sure you make the rows tall enough to write clearly in.

3 Label each row and column, and put the units in the headings so that you don't have to repeat them throughout the table.

Put the data in order so that the variable you're changing is getting bigger.

Temperature (°C)	Volume (cm^3)		
	Repeat 1	Repeat 2	Repeat 3
10			
20			
30			

Use sensible headings so that it's clear what each column and row is.

4 Fill in the rest of the table with the data.

Temperature (°C)	Volume (cm^3)		
	Repeat 1	Repeat 2	Repeat 3
10	32	28	37
20	60	47	51
30	70	68	72

There should be a number in every space.

Tables like this often have a final column to show the mean of the repeats. See p.2 for more on calculating means.

Drawing Tables

Now it's your turn. Here's some data from some experiments for you to practise putting into tables.

Q1 Some students were investigating how long a reaction took in seconds at three different temperatures: 10 °C, 20 °C and 30 °C. They repeated the experiment three times. Put their data into a table. **CHEMISTRY**

```
10 °C    20 °C    30 °C
31s      22s      10s
30s      19s      11s
29s      20s      11s
```

Q2 Milly investigated how effective two antibiotics (A and B) are. She applied each antibiotic to a paper disc and put the discs in a Petri dish of bacteria. After two days she measured the space that had been cleared around each disc. She repeated her experiment three times. Draw a table to display her data. **BIOLOGY**

```
  A      B          A      B          A      B
7 mm   1 mm       6 mm   3 mm       8 mm   2 mm
```

Q3 Some students are investigating how increasing the surface area of a parachute affects how long it takes to fall from a certain height. They repeat the experiment four times. Put their data below into a table. **PHYSICS**

```
25 cm²   36 cm²   49 cm²          25 cm²   36 cm²   49 cm²
 4.2 s    6.9 s    9.7 s           4.6 s    5.1 s    9.6 s

25 cm²   36 cm²   49 cm²          25 cm²   36 cm²   49 cm²
 4.3 s    7.2 s    9.5 s           4.4 s    7.1 s    9.3 s
```

Drawing Bar Charts

It's not too tricky to turn a table of data into a bar chart. You just need to draw the axes, work out how tall the bars need to be, and then you can get your colouring pencils out to finish the job. Nothing more to it.

Example

A student has recorded the mass of carbohydrate, protein and fat in two different foods. Draw a bar chart to show this data.

Food Group	Food A (g)	Food B (g)
Carbohydrate	18	22
Protein	29	17
Fat	6	12

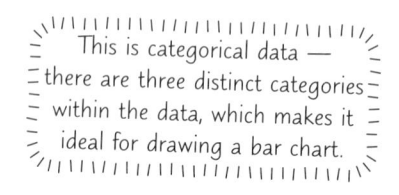

This is categorical data — there are three distinct categories within the data, which makes it ideal for drawing a bar chart.

1 Work out which variable needs to go on each axis, and whether you need a key.

The categories go on the x-axis — the one along the bottom.
The dependent variable (the thing that was measured for each category) goes on the y-axis — the one up the side.
If there's more than one set of data for each category, you'll need to use a key.

Food Group	Food A (g)	Food B (g)
Carbohydrate	18	22
Protein	29	17
Fat	6	12

These are the categories.

The mass of nutrient is the dependent variable — it's what was measured.

Here there are two sets of data for each category.

2 Choose a sensible scale for your axes and label them. You also need to make the x-axis long enough to leave a space between each category. The axes should fill at least half of the space that you're given.

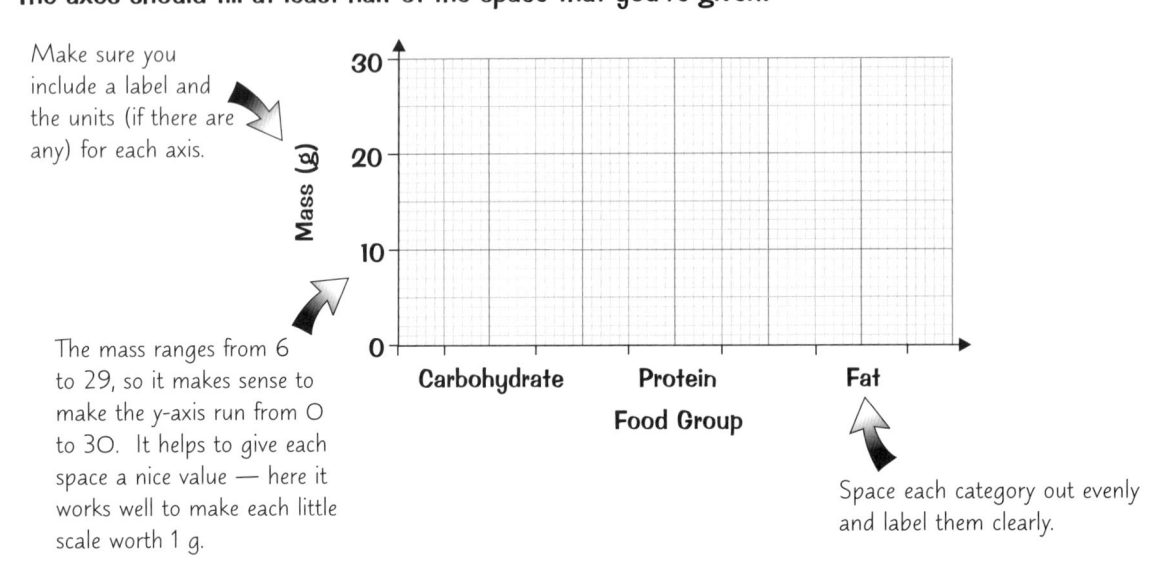

Make sure you include a label and the units (if there are any) for each axis.

The mass ranges from 6 to 29, so it makes sense to make the y-axis run from 0 to 30. It helps to give each space a nice value — here it works well to make each little scale worth 1 g.

Space each category out evenly and label them clearly.

Section 2 — Presenting Data

3) Draw the bars neatly with a sharp pencil. Make sure each bar is the same width.

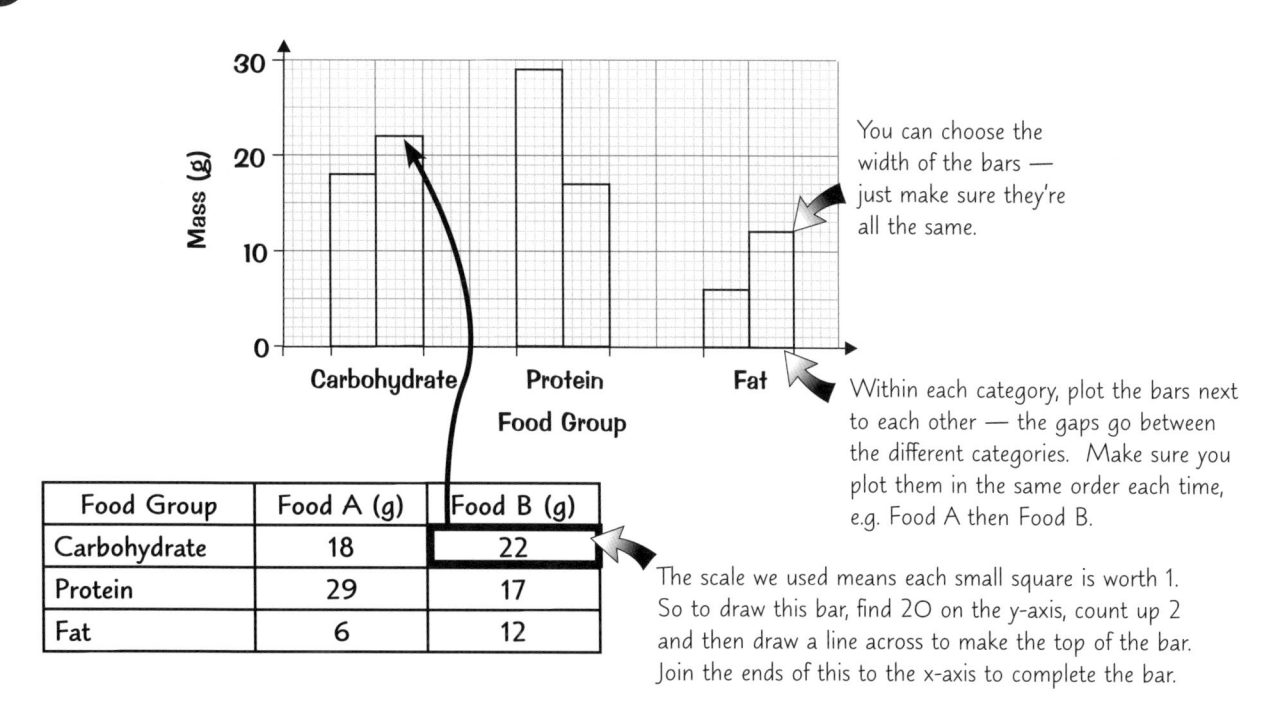

Food Group	Food A (g)	Food B (g)
Carbohydrate	18	22
Protein	29	17
Fat	6	12

You can choose the width of the bars — just make sure they're all the same.

Within each category, plot the bars next to each other — the gaps go between the different categories. Make sure you plot them in the same order each time, e.g. Food A then Food B.

The scale we used means each small square is worth 1. So to draw this bar, find 20 on the y-axis, count up 2 and then draw a line across to make the top of the bar. Join the ends of this to the x-axis to complete the bar.

4) If you have more than one set of data then shade the bars of each set differently and draw a key.

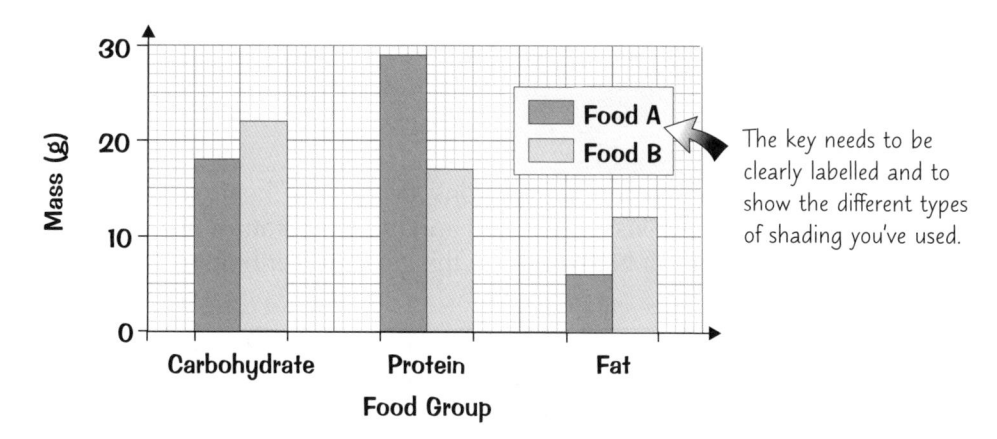

The key needs to be clearly labelled and to show the different types of shading you've used.

5) Shading in bars on a graph isn't as much fun as shading in cows...

Section 2 — Presenting Data

Drawing Bar Charts

It's time for you to turn some data tables into pretty bar charts. Sharpen your pencil and grab a ruler...

Q1 Chris carried out an experiment to find the energy content of four food samples. His results are in the table below. Draw a bar chart of his results on the graph paper. **BIOLOGY**

Food Sample	A	B	C	D
Energy (J/g)	29	11	37	16

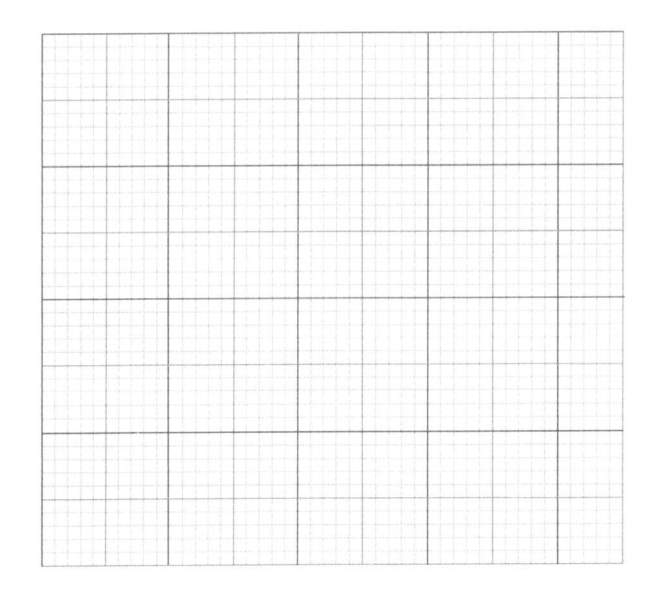

Q2 Gemma was investigating exothermic reactions for use in a 'heat pack'. Five different chemical reactions were tested and the temperature rise was recorded. Draw a bar chart of her results on the graph paper below. **CHEMISTRY**

Reaction	1	2	3	4	5
Temperature rise (°C)	10	21	53	17	26

Section 2 — Presenting Data

Q3 Liz carried out a survey on two year groups to find out students' weights. She then calculated the average weight for males and females in each year. Draw a bar chart of her results below on the graph paper.

BIOLOGY

	Average Weight (kg)	
Year	Male	Female
10	54	51
11	57	53

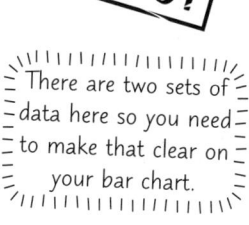

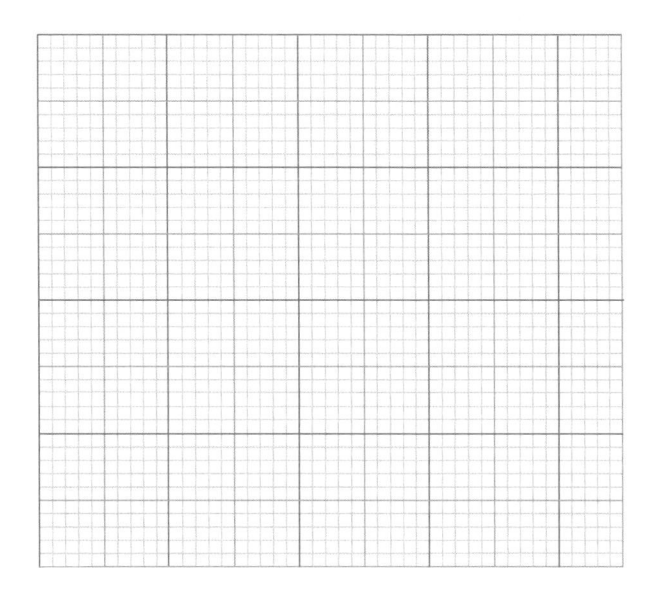

There are two sets of data here so you need to make that clear on your bar chart.

Q4 Some students were investigating the time taken for different balls to roll down two different ramps. They calculated the average time taken for each ball. Draw a bar chart of the results on the graph paper below.

PHYSICS

	Average time (s)		
Ramp	Ping pong ball	Golf ball	Tennis ball
A	2.4	1.9	2.1
B	3.2	2.5	2.8

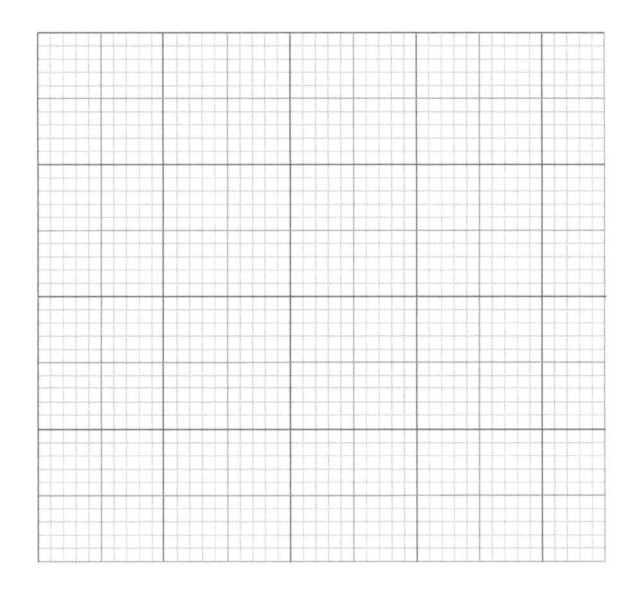

Section 2 — Presenting Data

Drawing Line Graphs

Drawing a line graph is just like doing a dot-to-dot — the difference is you have to draw the dots first before you can do the joining. On a serious note, line graphs are good for showing how things change over time.

Example

Some students recorded the highest temperature for the first ten days in November. Draw a line graph to show their data.

Day	1	2	3	4	5	6	7	8	9	10
Temperature (°C)	8	11	16	18	14	12	10	15	13	11

1 Work out which variable to put on each axis.

The independent variable (the thing that was changed) goes on the x-axis.
The dependent variable (the thing that was measured) goes on the y-axis.

Day	1	2	3	4	5	6	7	8	9	10
Temperature (°C)	8	11	16	18	14	12	10	15	13	11

This is the variable that was changed. (The time of each measurement was chosen.)

This is the variable that was measured.

2 Draw your axes so that they've got a sensible scale, and label them. The axes should fill up at least half of the space on the graph paper that you've been given.

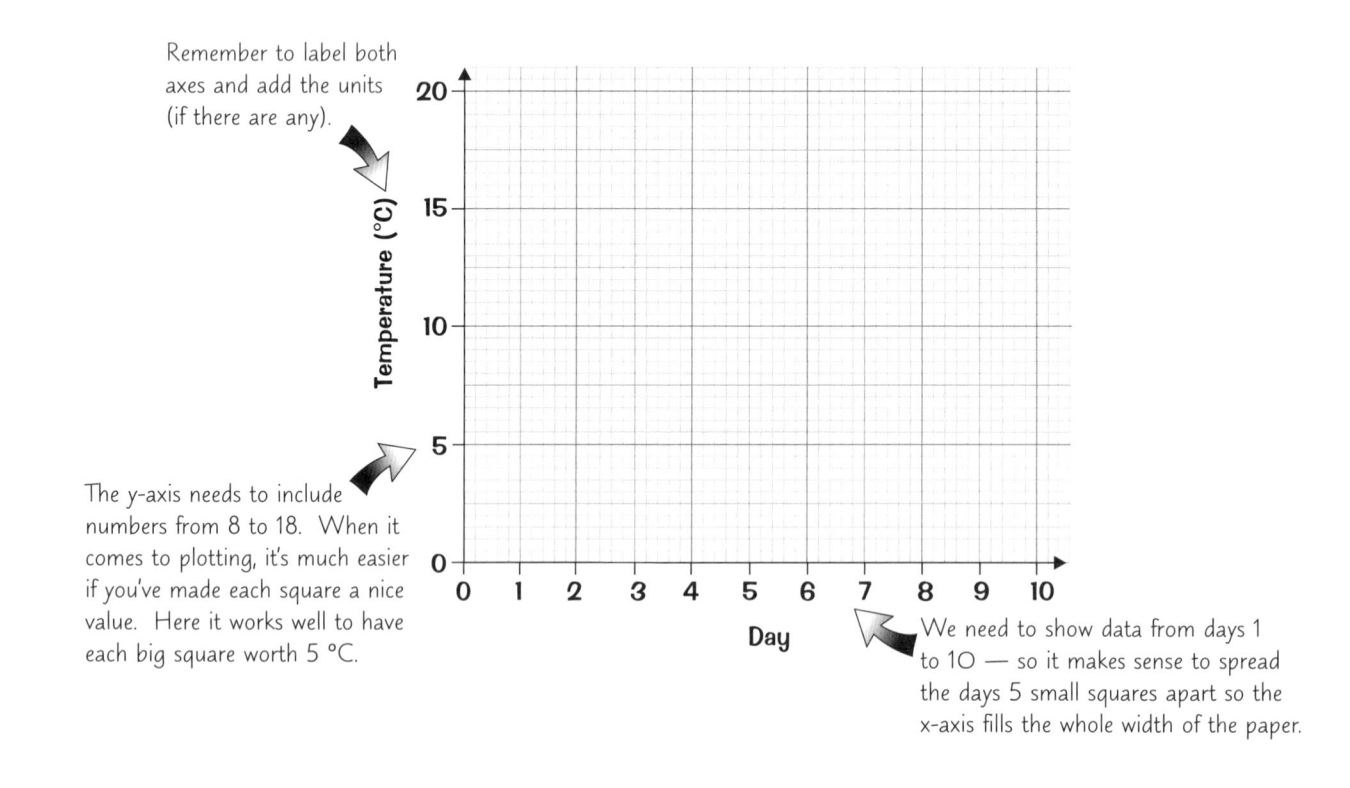

Remember to label both axes and add the units (if there are any).

The y-axis needs to include numbers from 8 to 18. When it comes to plotting, it's much easier if you've made each square a nice value. Here it works well to have each big square worth 5 °C.

We need to show data from days 1 to 10 — so it makes sense to spread the days 5 small squares apart so the x-axis fills the whole width of the paper.

Section 2 — Presenting Data

3) Plot the points with neat little crosses (not blobs). Make sure you use a sharp pencil.

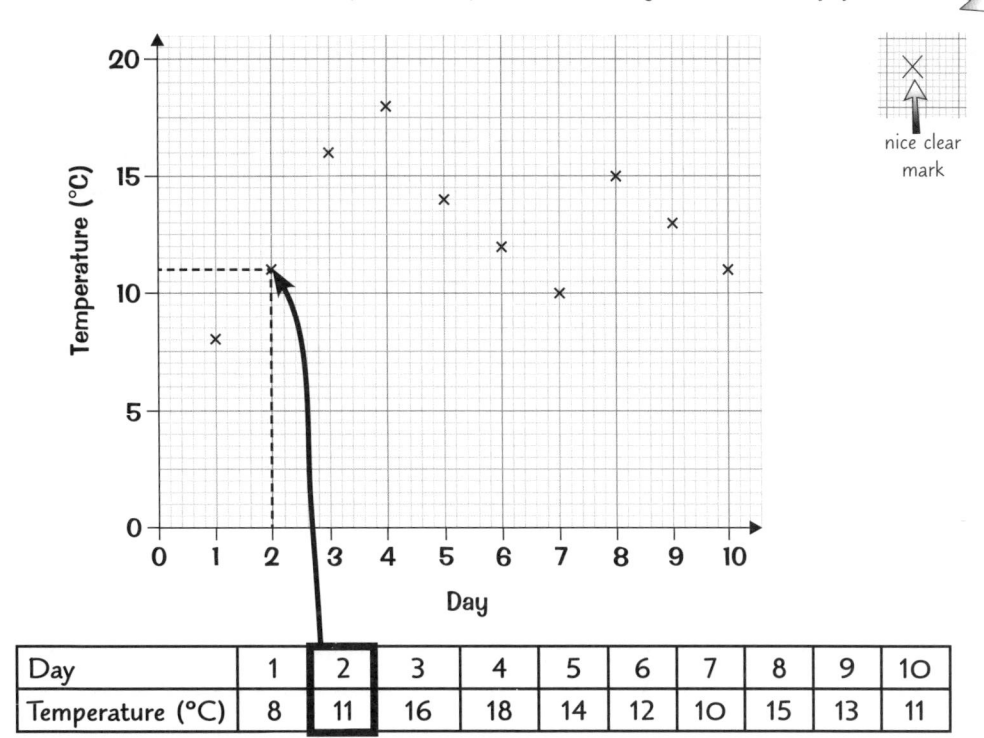

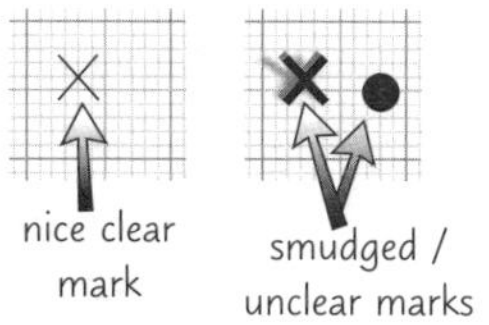

nice clear mark

smudged / unclear marks

Day	1	2	3	4	5	6	7	8	9	10
Temperature (°C)	8	11	16	18	14	12	10	15	13	11

The scale we used means each small square is worth 0.5 °C. So to plot this point, go across to day 2 on the x-axis and then count up 2 squares from 10 on the y-axis to get to 11, and make a neat cross there.

4) Use a ruler and a sharp pencil to draw straight lines connecting each point to the one next to it.

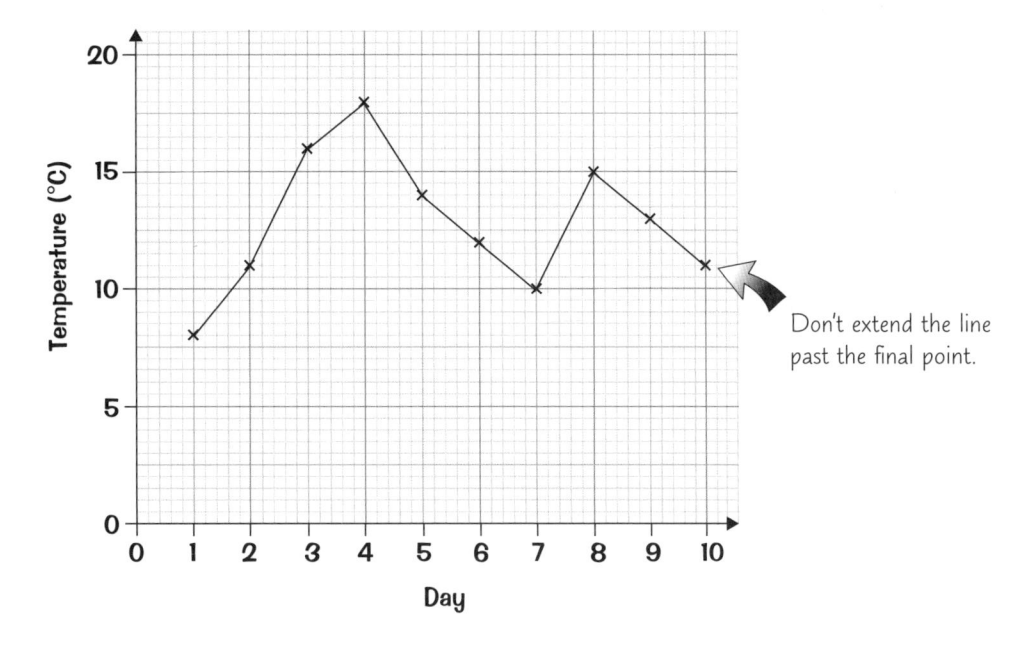

Don't extend the line past the final point.

5) If Step 4 brought back warm fuzzy memories of doing dot-to-dots then have a go at this.

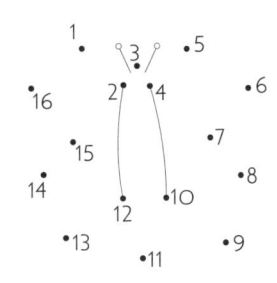

Section 2 — Presenting Data

Drawing Line Graphs

And now the fun begins... Get your ruler ready — it's time to draw some line graphs.

Q1 Some students investigated the distance a cyclist travelled over three hours. They recorded his distance at 30-minute intervals. Draw a line graph of the results below.

PHYSICS

Time (hours)	0	0.5	1.0	1.5	2.0	2.5	3.0
Distance (km)	0	12	25	30	44	58	70

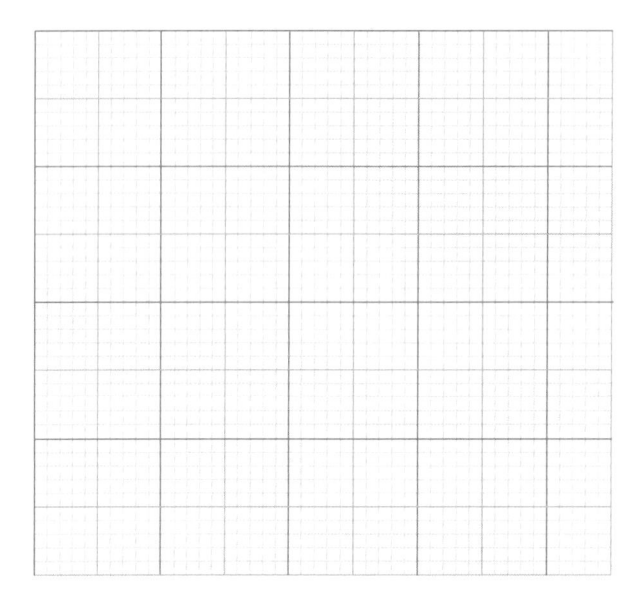

Q2 Noah calculated the average number of frogs in his pond each year for five years. Draw a line graph of his results on the graph paper below.

BIOLOGY

Year	1	2	3	4	5
Number of Frogs	6	10	7	14	20

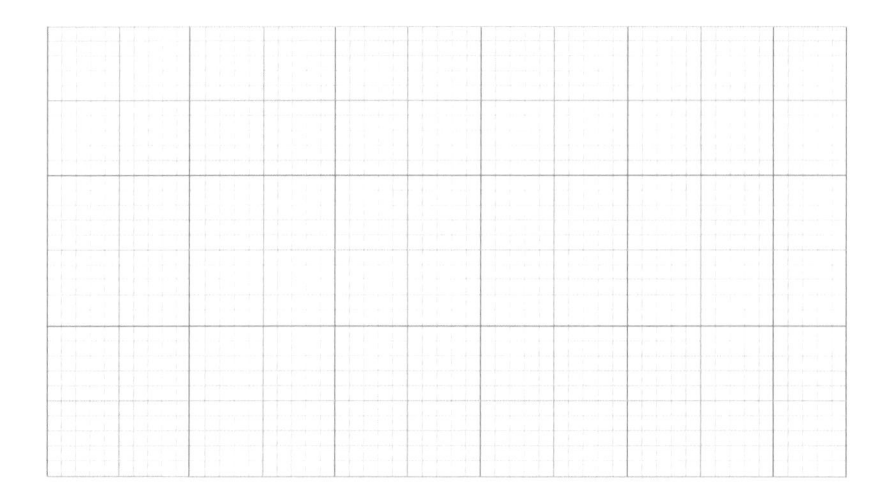

Section 2 — Presenting Data

Q3 Bernard wanted to plot the atomic number of the first 10 elements against their mass number. Draw a line graph of his data from the table below.

CHEMISTRY

Atomic Number	1	2	3	4	5	6	7	8	9	10
Mass Number	1	4	7	9	11	12	14	16	19	20

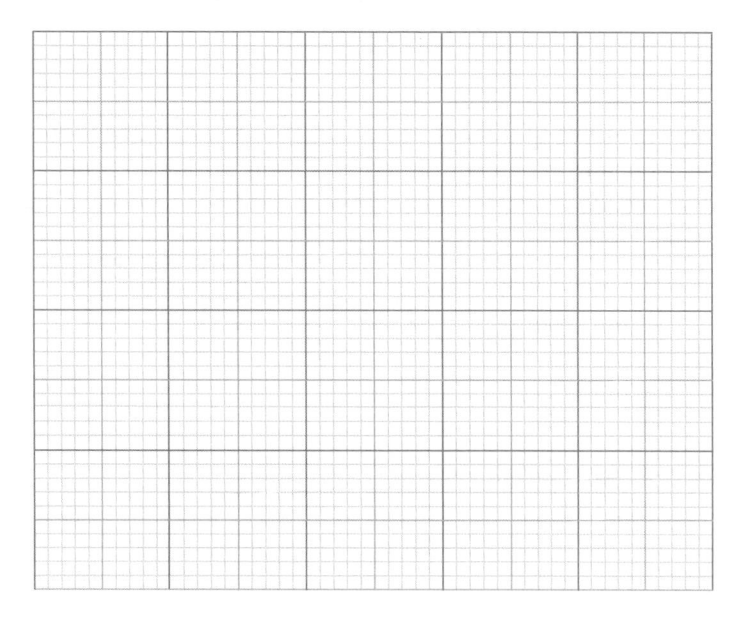

Q4 Ayla investigated how the height of a firework changes over time. Draw a line graph of her results on the graph paper below.

PHYSICS

Time (s)	0	1	2	3	4
Height (feet)	2	56	78	68	26

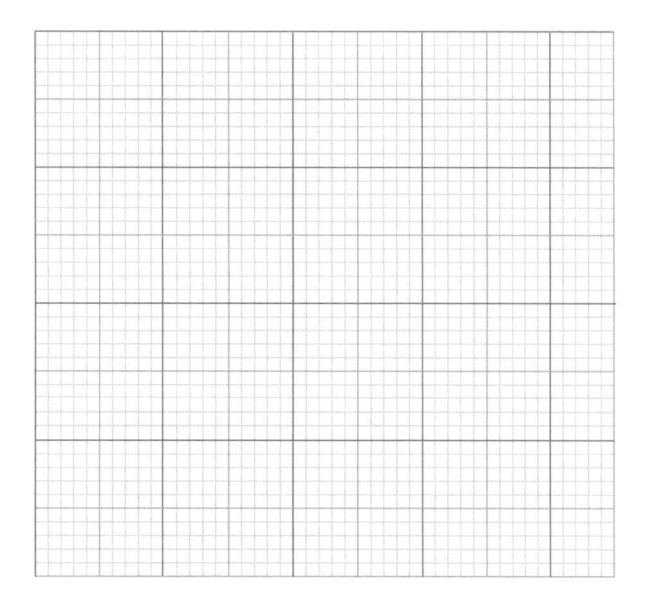

Section 2 — Presenting Data

Drawing Scatter Graphs

Raw data isn't much fun to look at. It's much nicer to gaze lovingly at a graph. Scatter graphs are like line graphs, but you don't join every dot together. Instead you get to draw a line of best fit. Scatter graphs are great at showing how two variables relate to each other — so both of your variables need to be numbers.

Example

Sophie was investigating the effect of concentration on the rate of a reaction.
She tested four different concentrations and timed how long it took to produce 20 cm³ of gas in each reaction. Her results are in the table below. Plot her data on a scatter graph.

Concentration (mol/dm³)	0.5	1.0	1.5	2.0
Time taken (s)	38	19	21	9

1 Decide which variable is going on each axis.

The independent variable (the thing that was changed) goes on the x-axis (across the bottom).
The dependent variable (the thing that was measured) goes on the y-axis (up the side).

Concentration (mol/dm³)	0.5	1.0	1.5	2.0
Time taken (s)	38	19	21	9

← This is the variable that was changed.

← This is the variable that was measured.

2 Draw your axes and label them. The axes should sensibly fill the space you're given and you should make each square of graph paper worth a nice value so it's easy to plot.

The time ranges from 9 to 38, so it makes sense to make the y-axis run from 0 to 40. The graph paper is 4 big squares tall, so if we start at 0 and make each large square worth 10 it will take 4 squares to get to 40. Nice.

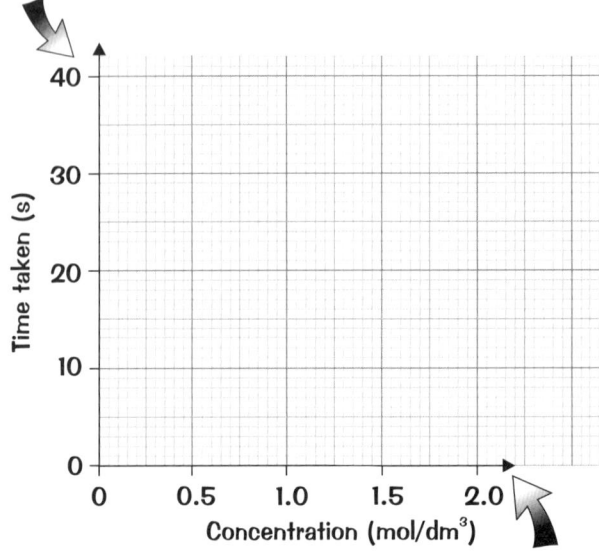

Concentration goes on the bottom and the data range is 0.5 to 2.0. The graph paper is 5 big squares wide. So 4 squares each worth 0.5 seems a sensible scale.

3 Plot the points using a sharp pencil and make neat little crosses (<u>not</u> blobs).

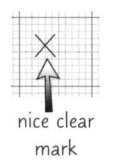

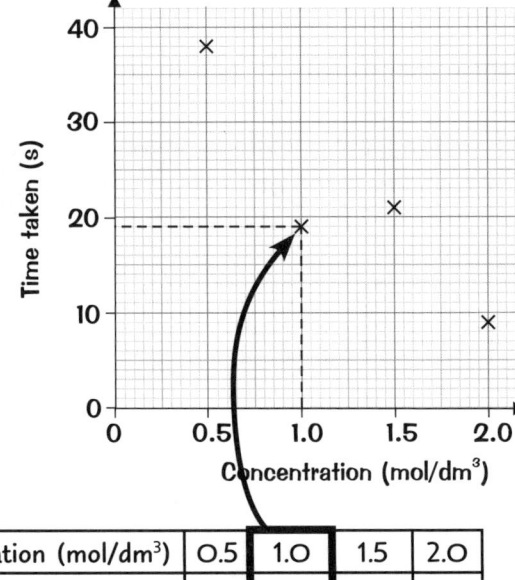

nice clear mark

smudged / unclear marks

Concentration (mol/dm³)	0.5	1.0	1.5	2.0
Time taken (s)	38	19	21	9

The scale we used means each small square on the y-axis is worth 1. So to plot this point go across to 1.0 on the x-axis and then count up 9 squares from 10 on the y-axis to get 19, and put a neat cross there.

4 Then draw a line of best fit — a line that passes through, or as near as possible to, as many of the points as you can. These help to show any trends in the data. Ignore anomalous results when drawing them.

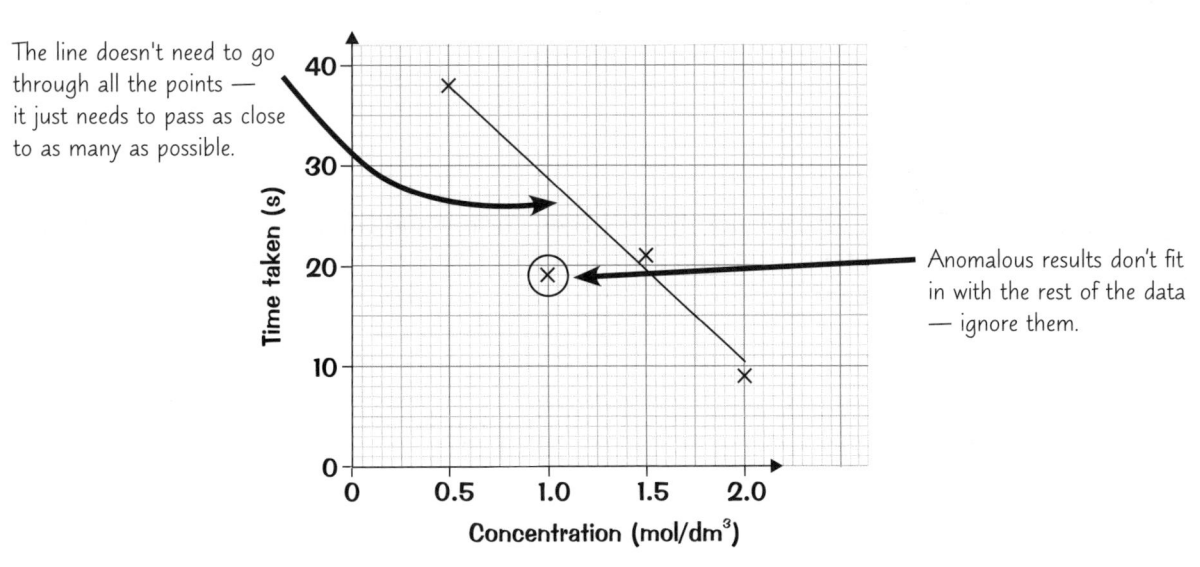

The line doesn't need to go through all the points — it just needs to pass as close to as many as possible.

Anomalous results don't fit in with the rest of the data — ignore them.

5 Sometimes your points will follow a curved pattern and so you'll need to draw a curved line of best fit.

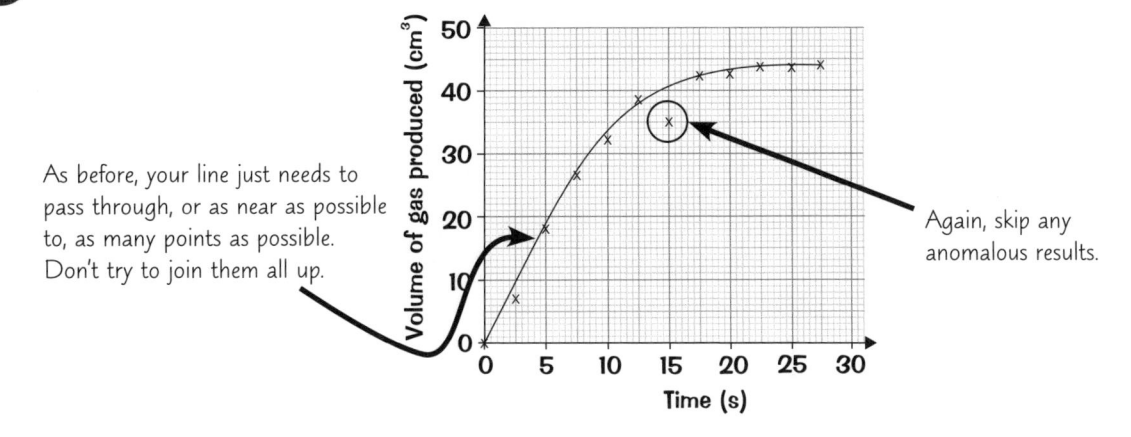

As before, your line just needs to pass through, or as near as possible to, as many points as possible. Don't try to join them all up.

Again, skip any anomalous results.

Section 2 — Presenting Data

Drawing Scatter Graphs

Right, your turn. Here's some data from some experiments for you to practise plotting on a scatter graph.

Q1 Ash carried out an experiment to investigate how temperature affects the rate of a reaction. Plot a scatter graph of his results on the graph paper below. Draw a line of best fit on your graph.

CHEMISTRY

Temperature (°C)	0	5	10	15	20	25	30
Rate of Reaction (cm³/s)	0	3	7	8	17	16	19

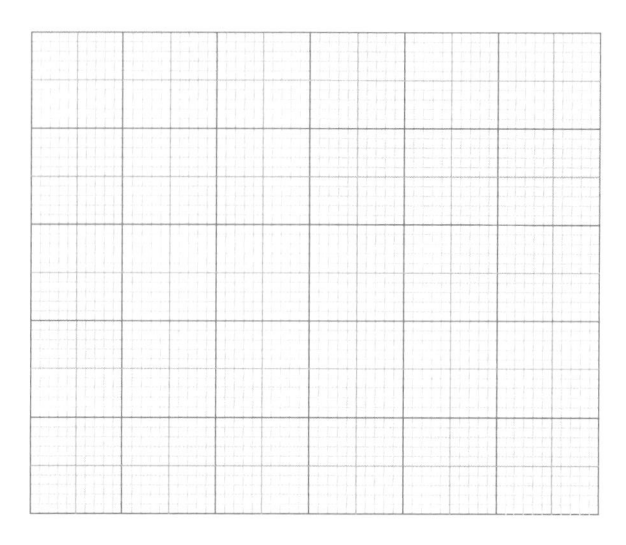

Q2 Lara was investigating the relationship between current and voltage. Plot a scatter graph of her results on the graph paper below. Include a line of best fit.

PHYSICS

Current (A)	2	3	4	5	6	7	8	9	10
Voltage (V)	1.9	3.2	3.8	5.0	5.8	7.2	7.8	8.4	9.8

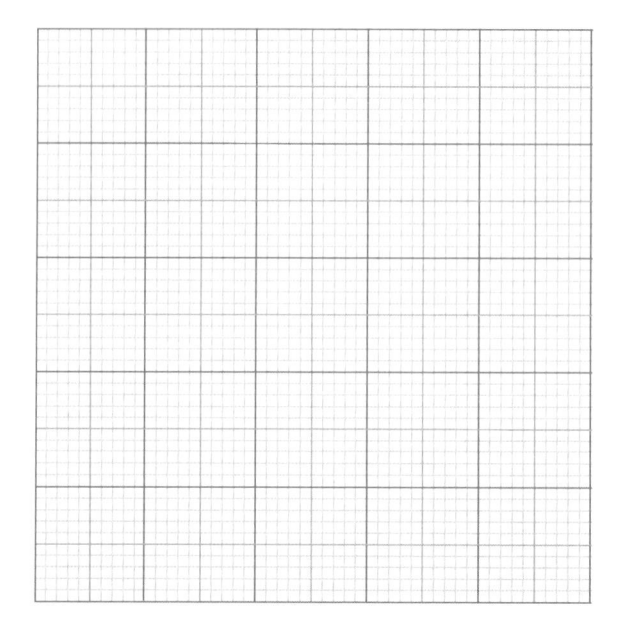

Section 2 — Presenting Data

Q3 Paul was investigating the relationship between temperature and rate of reaction. He used a chemical reaction where the contents of the beaker became cloudy over time. He measured the rate of reaction by timing how long it took for a mark under the beaker to disappear from view. Plot a scatter graph of his results below and draw a line of best fit.

CHEMISTRY

Temperature (°C)	10	20	30	40	50
Time taken for mark to disappear (s)	195	150	110	85	50

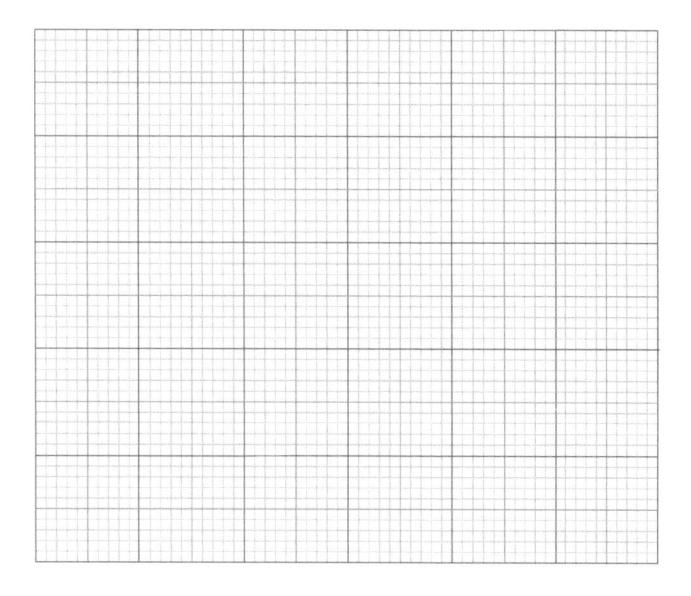

Q4 Some students were investigating the effect of light intensity on the rate of photosynthesis of pondweed in a beaker of water. The light intensity was varied by placing a lamp at different distances from the plant. The rate of photosynthesis was measured by counting how many bubbles of gas were produced in one minute. Plot a scatter graph of the results below and draw a line of best fit.

BIOLOGY

Distance (cm)	0	5	10	15	20	25	30	35	40	45	50
Bubbles per minute	245	210	185	155	120	90	65	50	40	25	20

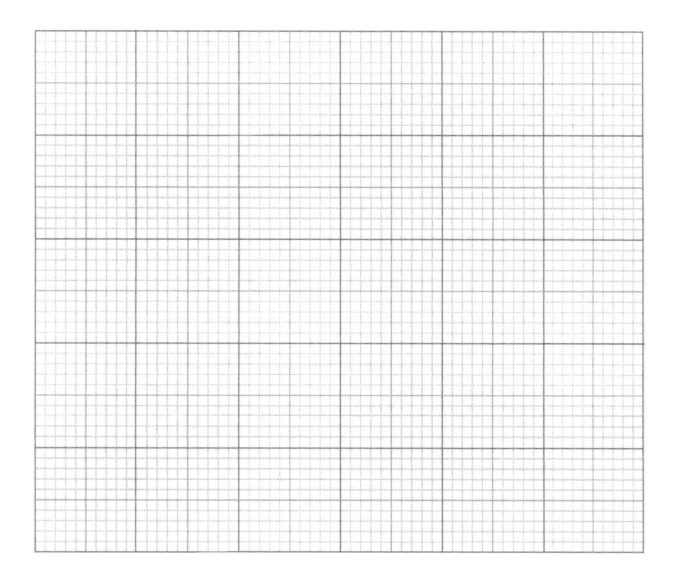

Section 2 — Presenting Data

Drawing Pie Charts

Pie charts are not the best type of pie, but they're a good way of displaying data that falls into categories. They take a bit more work than other graphs and charts as you have to work out the angle for each category, but it's worth it for the pretty picture you end up with. Just don't expect it to taste good.

Example

Josh recorded the mass of different food groups in one type of food. His results are shown in the table below. Draw a pie chart of the results.

Food Group	Mass (g)
Carbohydrate	7
Protein	10
Fat	5
Fibre	6
Other	2

1 Add up all the numbers to get the total.

$$7 + 10 + 5 + 6 + 2 = 30$$

So the total mass of the food is 30 g.

2 Divide 360 by the total from Step 1.

There are 360° in a circle. $$360 \div 30 = 12$$ This means that each gram is represented by 12° on the pie chart.

3 Multiply the value for each category by the number from Step 2. This gives the angle you need to draw for each category.

Food Group	Mass (g)	Angle (°)
Carbohydrate	7	7 × 12 = 84
Protein	10	10 × 12 = 120
Fat	5	5 × 12 = 60
Fibre	6	6 × 12 = 72
Other	2	2 × 12 = 24

It's useful to add an extra column to the table, where you can work out the angles.

This is the number we worked out in Step 2.

Section 2 — Presenting Data

4) Draw a circle using a compass and draw a start line up from the centre. Then measure the angle of the first category and draw another line to make a sector.

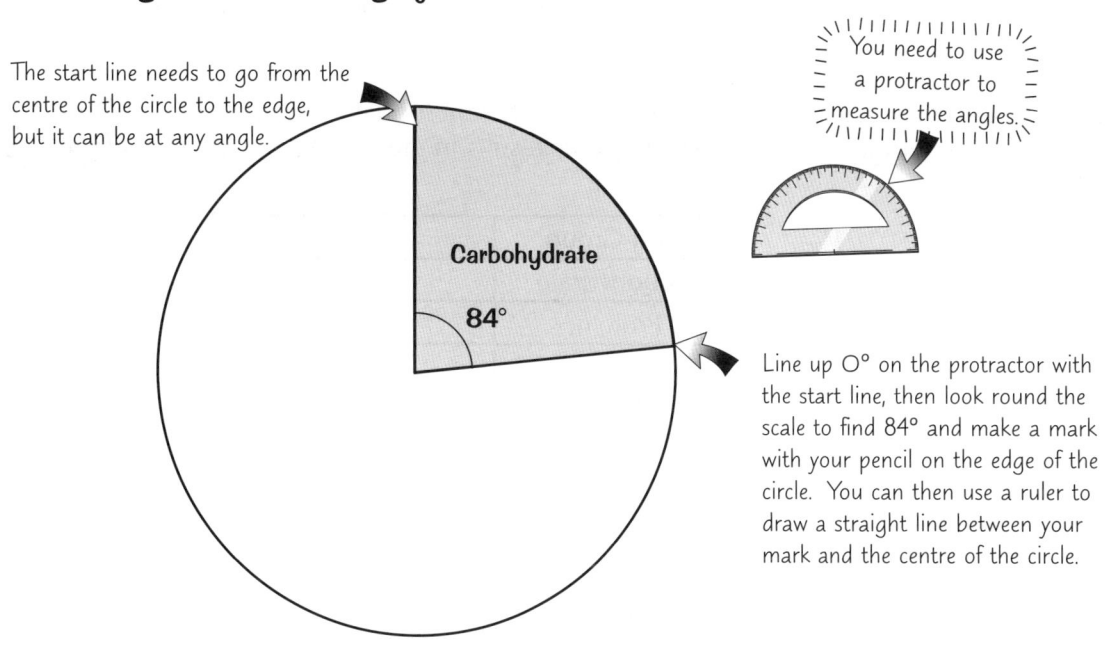

The start line needs to go from the centre of the circle to the edge, but it can be at any angle.

Carbohydrate 84°

You need to use a protractor to measure the angles.

Line up 0° on the protractor with the start line, then look round the scale to find 84° and make a mark with your pencil on the edge of the circle. You can then use a ruler to draw a straight line between your mark and the centre of the circle.

5) Starting from the line you drew for the first category, draw the rest of the angles onto the circle. Label each sector with the category that it represents.

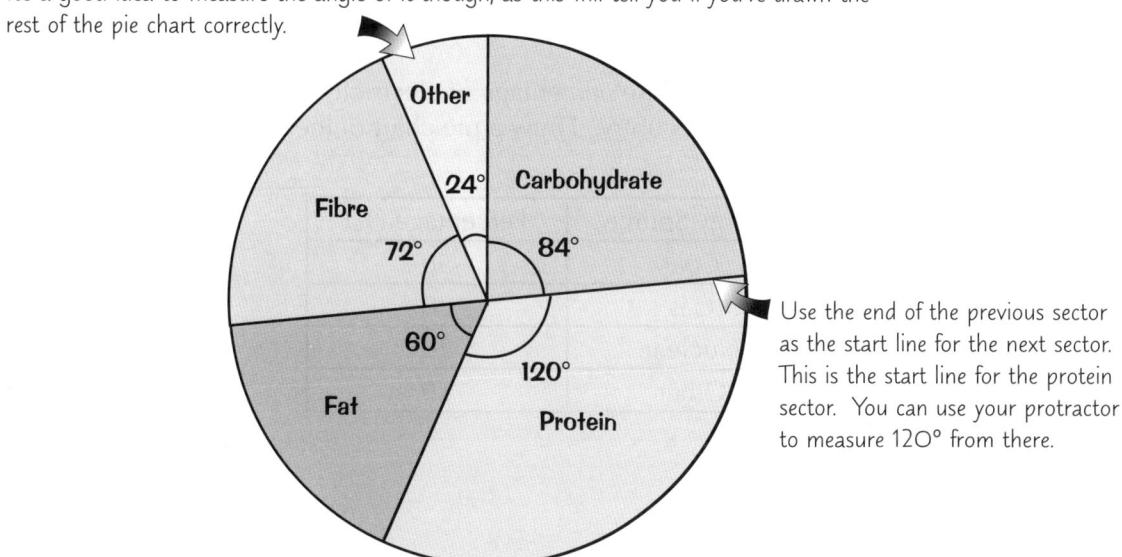

You won't need to draw the last sector, as it'll already be there after you've drawn the others. It's a good idea to measure the angle of it though, as this will tell you if you've drawn the rest of the pie chart correctly.

Other 24°
Carbohydrate 84°
Fibre 72°
Fat 60°
Protein 120°

Use the end of the previous sector as the start line for the next sector. This is the start line for the protein sector. You can use your protractor to measure 120° from there.

6) Enough about pies. Try running like a slug.

Section 2 — Presenting Data

Drawing Pie Charts

Make sure you've got a protractor handy — you're going to need it to draw some pie charts from this data.

Q1 George was investigating the mass of different food groups in one type of food. Draw a pie chart of his results in the space below.

BIOLOGY

You might want to add an extra column to the table so that you've got somewhere to work out the angles.

Food Group	Mass (g)
Carbohydrate	40
Protein	6
Fat	5
Fibre	7
Other	2

Q2 Some students were investigating the percentage of electricity produced by various energy sources in their country. Draw a pie chart of their results.

PHYSICS

Energy Source	Percentage (%)
Coal	50
Gas	20
Nuclear	20
Other	10

Section 2 — Presenting Data

Q3 The masses of the elements in CaCO$_3$ are given in the table below in terms of their percentage of the mass of the whole compound. Draw a pie chart to show this data.

CHEMISTRY

Element	Percentage (%)
Calcium	40
Carbon	12
Oxygen	48

Q4 Richard did a survey to find out how much exercise people do in a week. Draw a pie chart of his results in the space below.

BIOLOGY

Exercise Time	Number of People
Less than 1 hour	10
1-2 hours	4
3-4 hours	9
5-6 hours	4
More than 6 hours	3

Section 2 — Presenting Data

Drawing Histograms

Histograms may look like innocent bar charts, but don't be fooled — they've got a few hidden depths. Luckily you've got these nice steps to follow and before you know it you'll be drawing them in your sleep.

Example

Ali was investigating the length of beetles in her garden.
Draw a histogram of her results in the table below.

Length (mm)	Frequency
$0 < x \leq 10$	32
$10 < x \leq 15$	36
$15 < x \leq 18$	24
$18 < x \leq 22$	28
$22 < x \leq 30$	16

1 Work out the class width of each class by subtracting the smallest number in each class from the largest number.

Length (mm)	Frequency	Class Width
$0 < x \leq 10$	32	$10 - 0 = 10$
$10 < x \leq 15$	36	$15 - 10 = 5$
$15 < x \leq 18$	24	$18 - 15 = 3$
$18 < x \leq 22$	28	$22 - 18 = 4$
$22 < x \leq 30$	16	$30 - 22 = 8$

It's this column of numbers that's used to work out the class widths.

It's useful to add another column to do this working in.

Each of these groups of lengths is known as a class.

2 Divide the frequency of each class by the class width to work out frequency density.

Length (mm)	Frequency	Class Width	Frequency Density
$0 < x \leq 10$	32	$10 - 0 = 10$	$32 \div 10 = 3.2$
$10 < x \leq 15$	36	$15 - 10 = 5$	$36 \div 5 = 7.2$
$15 < x \leq 18$	24	$18 - 15 = 3$	$24 \div 3 = 8$
$18 < x \leq 22$	28	$22 - 18 = 4$	$28 \div 4 = 7$
$22 < x \leq 30$	16	$30 - 22 = 8$	$16 \div 8 = 2$

Again, adding another column to work out the frequency density is a good idea. You're less likely to make a mistake if you write out your working.

Frequency   Class width

3 Draw your axes with a sensible scale and label them. The axes should take up at least half of the space on the graph paper you've been given. Always draw frequency density on the y-axis and the classes on the x-axis.

Frequency density always goes on the side.

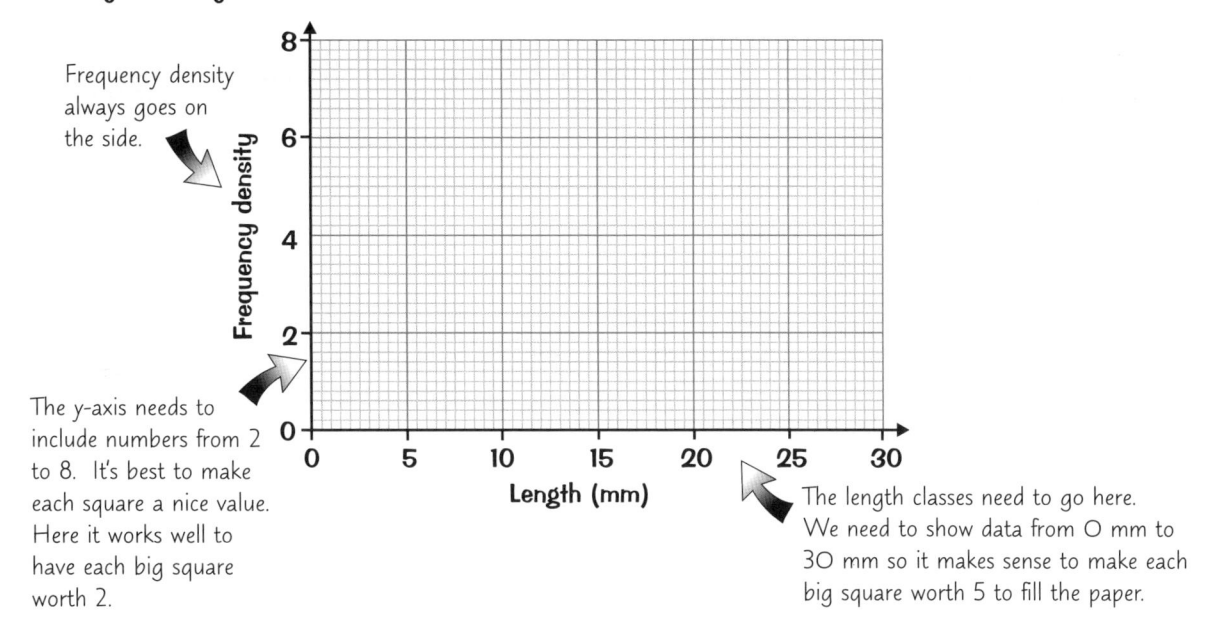

The y-axis needs to include numbers from 2 to 8. It's best to make each square a nice value. Here it works well to have each big square worth 2.

The length classes need to go here. We need to show data from 0 mm to 30 mm so it makes sense to make each big square worth 5 to fill the paper.

4 Draw the bars neatly with a sharp pencil. Each bar needs to be as wide as the class it is representing.

You can shade the bars to make them stand out more on the graph paper.

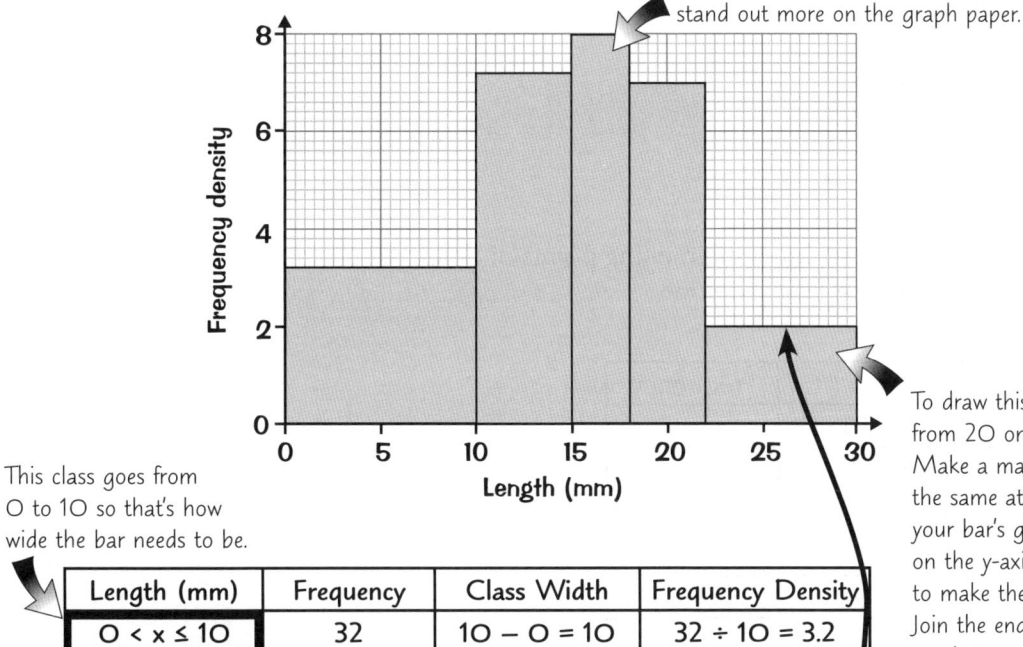

This class goes from 0 to 10 so that's how wide the bar needs to be.

To draw this bar, count along from 20 on the x-axis to find 22. Make a mark on the axis, then do the same at 30. That's how wide your bar's got to be. Then find 2 on the y-axis and draw a line to make the top of the bar. Join the ends of this to the x-axis to complete the bar.

Length (mm)	Frequency	Class Width	Frequency Density
$0 < x \leq 10$	32	$10 - 0 = 10$	$32 \div 10 = 3.2$
$10 < x \leq 15$	36	$15 - 10 = 5$	$36 \div 5 = 7.2$
$15 < x \leq 18$	24	$18 - 15 = 3$	$24 \div 3 = 8$
$18 < x \leq 22$	28	$22 - 18 = 4$	$28 \div 4 = 7$
$22 < x \leq 30$	16	$30 - 22 = 8$	$16 \div 8 = 2$

Section 2 — Presenting Data

Drawing Histograms

Grab a ruler and a calculator and get stuck into these questions. You might just learn to love histograms...

Q1 Some students were investigating the height of apple trees in an orchard. Draw a histogram of their results below.

BIOLOGY

Height (m)	Frequency
$0 < x \leq 2$	38
$2 < x \leq 3.5$	30
$3.5 < x \leq 4$	22
$4 < x \leq 4.5$	18
$4.5 < x \leq 6$	15

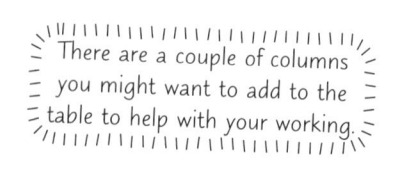

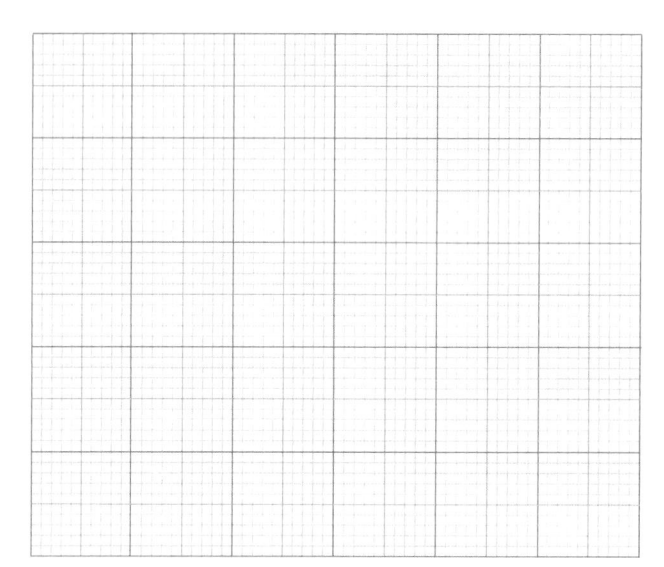

There are a couple of columns you might want to add to the table to help with your working.

Q2 Some students are investigating the melting points of different substances. Draw a histogram of the results below.

PHYSICS

Melting Point (°C)	Frequency
$0 < x \leq 15$	6
$15 < x \leq 30$	9
$30 < x \leq 40$	13
$40 < x \leq 50$	11
$50 < x \leq 70$	16

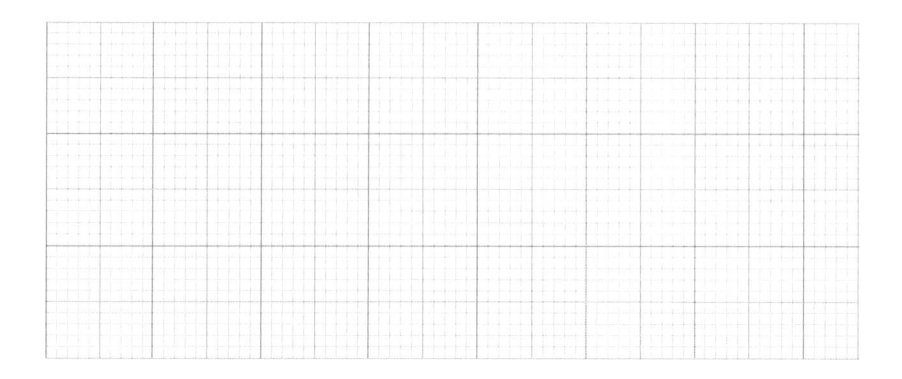

Section 2 — Presenting Data

Q3 Draw a histogram of the data below. CHEMISTRY

Concentration (g/l)	Frequency
$0 < x \le 0.4$	2
$0.4 < x \le 1.0$	9
$1.0 < x \le 1.2$	10
$1.2 < x \le 1.6$	16
$1.6 < x \le 2.4$	4

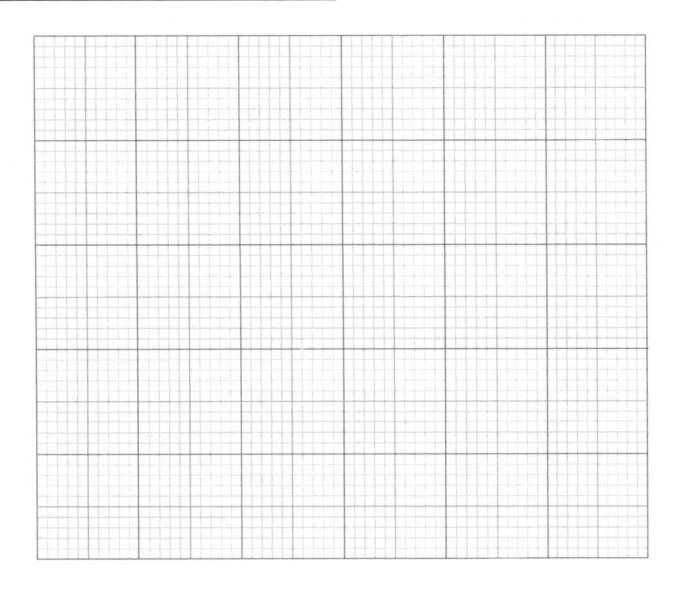

Q4 Ellie did an investigation into body temperature. Draw a histogram of her results below. BIOLOGY

Body Temperature (°C)	Frequency
$35.5 < x \le 36.5$	5
$36.5 < x \le 36.75$	2
$36.75 < x \le 37.25$	5
$37.25 < x \le 37.5$	1
$37.5 < x \le 38.5$	1

Section 2 — Presenting Data

Section 3 — Analysing Data

Interpreting Tables

When data is laid out nicely in a table, it makes it easier to find the information you want to know. You'd be searching through the raw data for ages otherwise. Figuring out tables is easy when you know how...

Example

Three groups of plants were treated with different fertilisers and left to grow for three weeks. Which fertiliser was the most effective?

Fertiliser	A	B	C
Mean Growth (mm)	13.5	19.5	5.5

1 Find the row or column that contains the measurements you're looking for.

Fertiliser	A	B	C
Mean Growth (mm)	13.5	19.5	5.5

The question asks you to compare plant growth, so this is the row you'll need to look at.

2 Pick out the piece of information the question is asking for.

Fertiliser	A	**B**	C
Mean Growth (mm)	13.5	**19.5**	5.5

You're looking for the largest number in the row, which is 19.5 mm — so fertiliser B was the most effective.

Example

Derek did a survey to find out how much exercise his classmates did in a week. His results are in the table below. How many students did less than 2 hours of exercise during the week?

Time (mins)	0 - 59	60 - 119	120 - 179	180 +
Number of students	11	16	9	13

1 Find the row or column that contains the measurements you're looking for.

Time (mins)	0 - 59	60 - 119	120 - 179	180 +
Number of students	11	16	9	13

The question asks you to look at the time the students spent exercising, so this is the row you need to look at first.

2 Pick out the pieces of information the question is asking for.

Time (mins)	**0 - 59**	**60 - 119**	120 - 179	180 +
Number of students	**11**	**16**	9	13

You're only interested in the students who did less than 2 hours of exercise, so that's the first two columns.

3 Add them together to get the total.

Time (mins)	0 - 59	60 - 119
Number of students	11	16

Total = 11 + 16 = 27 students

Interpreting Tables

Aaaaand now it's your turn. Here are some tables full of data, just waiting to be read...

Q1 Three catalysts were tested for their effectiveness in a particular chemical reaction. The results are in the table below. **CHEMISTRY**

Catalyst	Rate of Reaction (cm³/s)
A	17.5
B	10.5
C	4.5

a) Which catalyst gave the highest rate of reaction?

b) What was the difference between the highest rate of reaction and the lowest rate of reaction?

Q2 The table below shows some information about the different energy sources used to generate electricity. **PHYSICS**

	Coal	Gas	Nuclear	Wind
Efficiency	36%	50%	38%	35%
Energy output per year (millions of units)	8000	5000	7000	150
CO_2 emissions per unit	920	440	110	none
Average cost of energy per unit (p)	2.5	2	5	3

If a big table full of data is thrown at you, don't panic — just figure out what information the question wants and ignore the rest.

a) Which energy source has the highest average cost per unit?

b) What is the difference in CO_2 emissions per unit between coal and gas energy?

Q3 Two crops were grown in different fields and their yield was recorded each year. **BIOLOGY**

Yield (tonnes)	Crop A	Crop B
Year 1	7.5	6.5
Year 2	6.5	6.0
Year 3	8.0	5.0
Year 4	7.0	6.5
Year 5	8.5	7.5

a) What was the total yield of crop A over the first three years?

b) What was the total crop yield in the fifth year?

Section 3 — Analysing Data

Interpreting Bar Charts

Bar charts are really useful for comparing data, and they're way prettier than tables.

Example

A student was comparing how much energy four different activities use. The results are shown in this bar chart.

How much energy per minute does swimming use up?

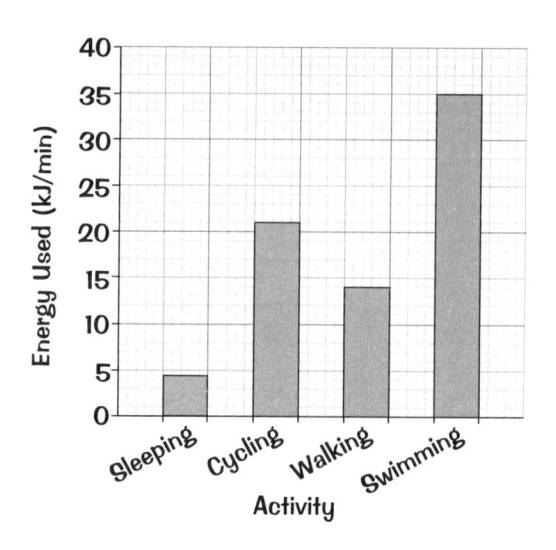

1 Pick the bar you need to look at.

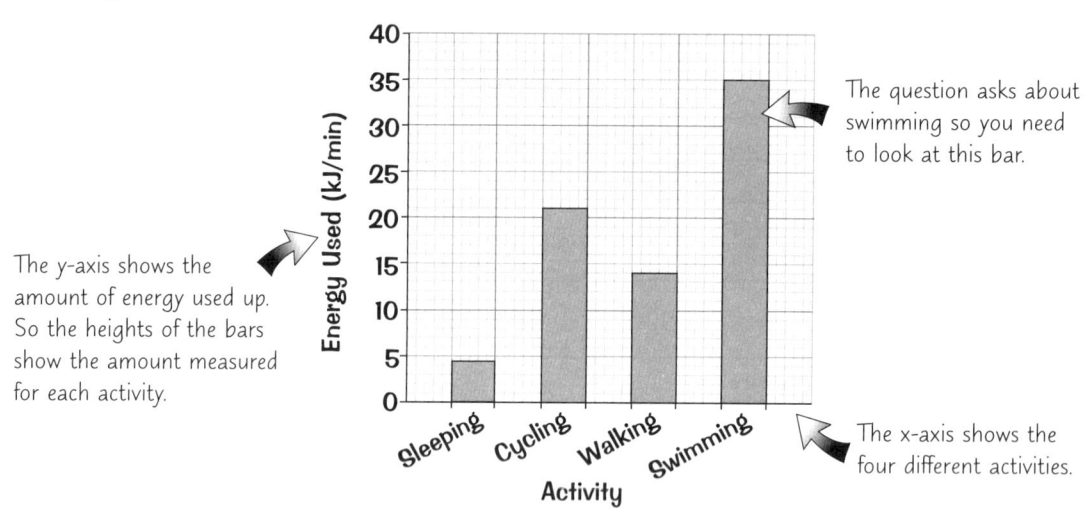

The question asks about swimming so you need to look at this bar.

The y-axis shows the amount of energy used up. So the heights of the bars show the amount measured for each activity.

The x-axis shows the four different activities.

2 Read across from the height of the bar to the value on the y-axis.

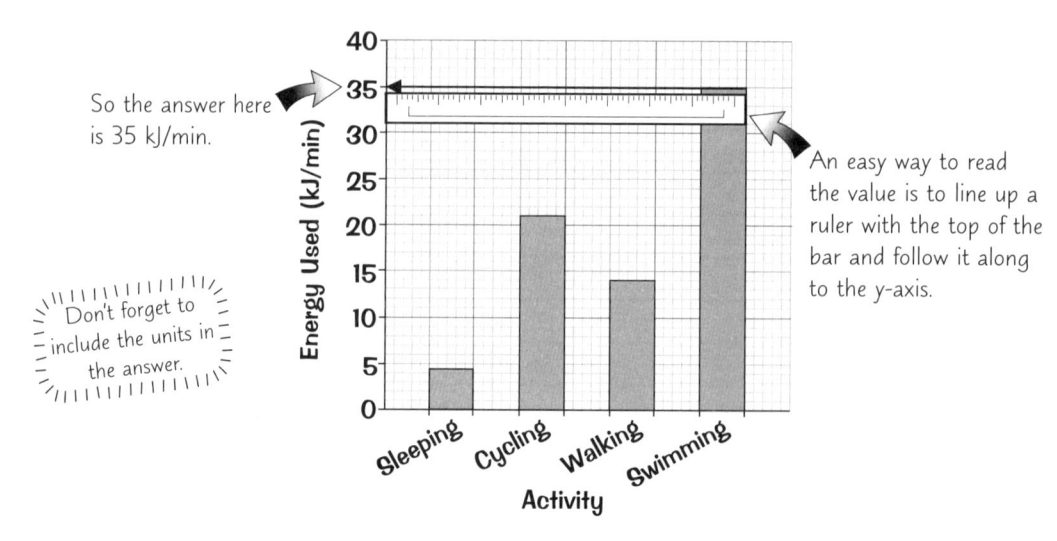

So the answer here is 35 kJ/min.

An easy way to read the value is to line up a ruler with the top of the bar and follow it along to the y-axis.

Don't forget to include the units in the answer.

3 Time to limbo.

Section 3 — Analysing Data

Example

The percentages of dark- and light-coloured moths in two different towns are shown in the bar chart opposite.

What is the difference between the percentages of dark-coloured moths in town A and town B?

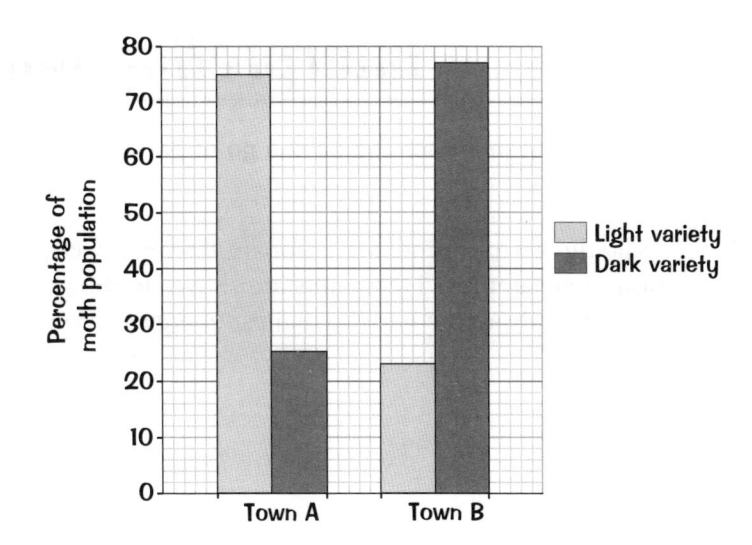

1 Pick the bars you need to look at.

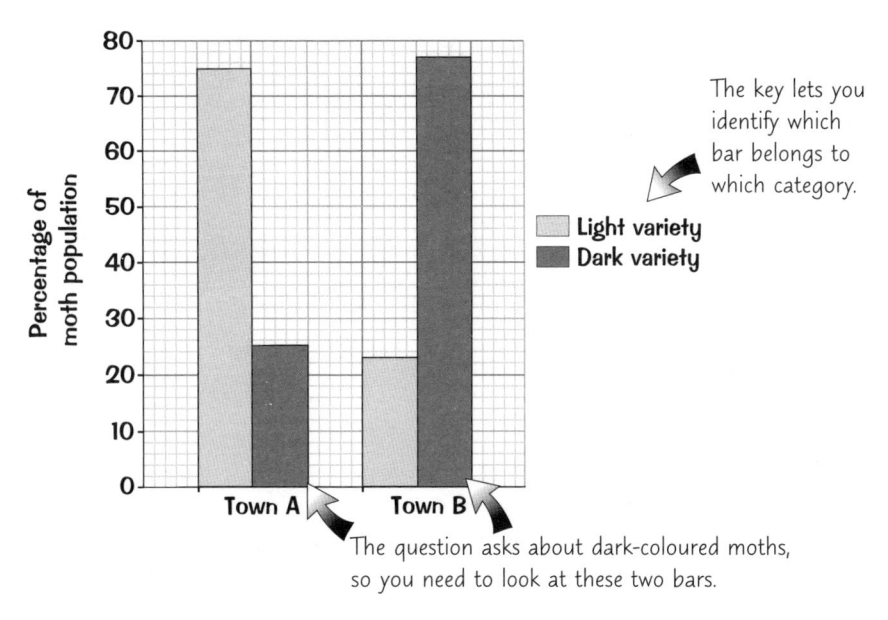

The key lets you identify which bar belongs to which category.

The question asks about dark-coloured moths, so you need to look at these two bars.

2 Read the values from the y-axis.

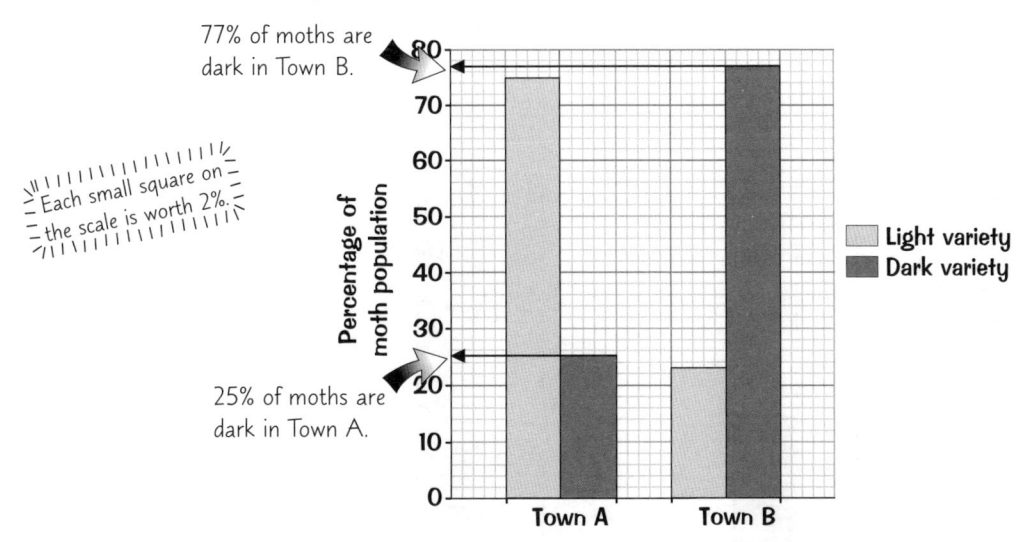

77% of moths are dark in Town B.

Each small square on the scale is worth 2%.

25% of moths are dark in Town A.

3 Subtract the smaller value from the bigger one to find the difference.

77% − 25% = 52%

Section 3 — Analysing Data

Interpreting Bar Charts

Right, your turn. Grab a ruler and have a go at getting the info out of these bar charts.

Q1 Julie did an experiment to compare the energy content of four fuel samples. Her results are shown in the graph below. Which fuel sample had the highest energy content?

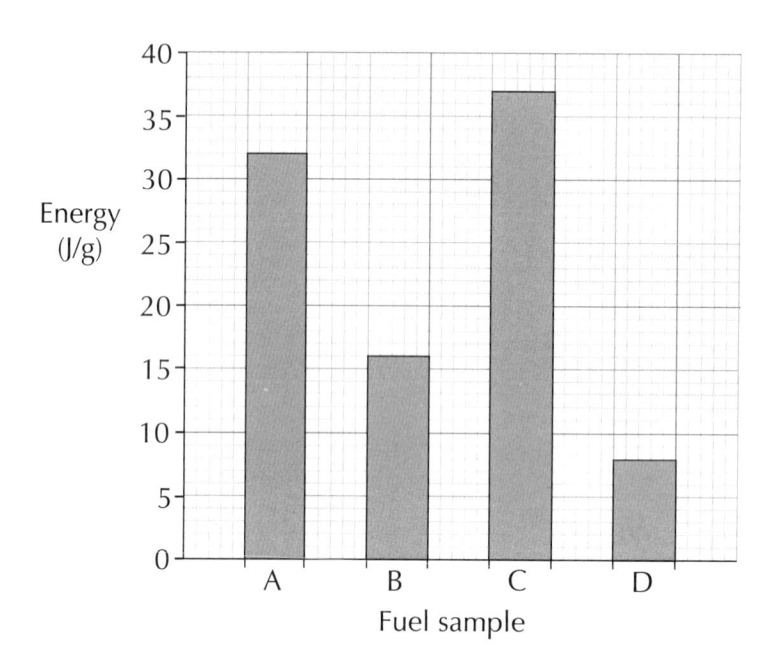

CHEMISTRY

Q2 The fat content of butter and olive oil were investigated and the results displayed in a graph. How much more saturated fat does butter have compared to olive oil?

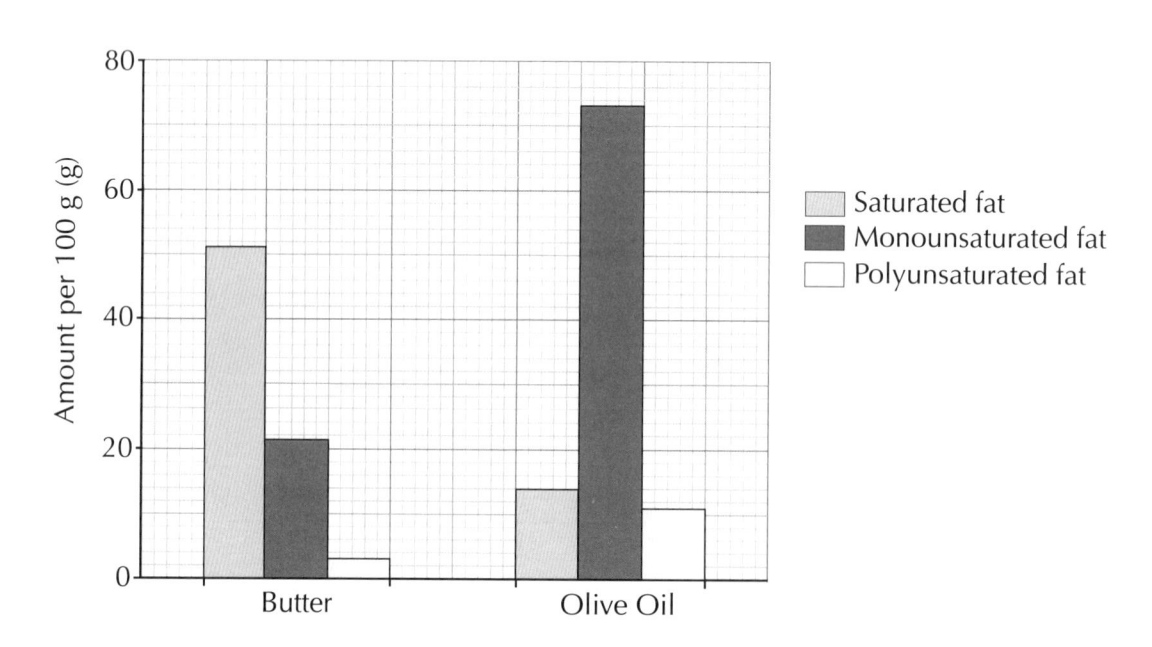

BIOLOGY

Section 3 — Analysing Data

Q3 Yvonne carried out an experiment to compare the amounts of water and humus in two different soil samples. She heated the samples twice — once at 105 °C and again at 550 °C. How much more mass did sample A lose after the two heating stages than sample B?

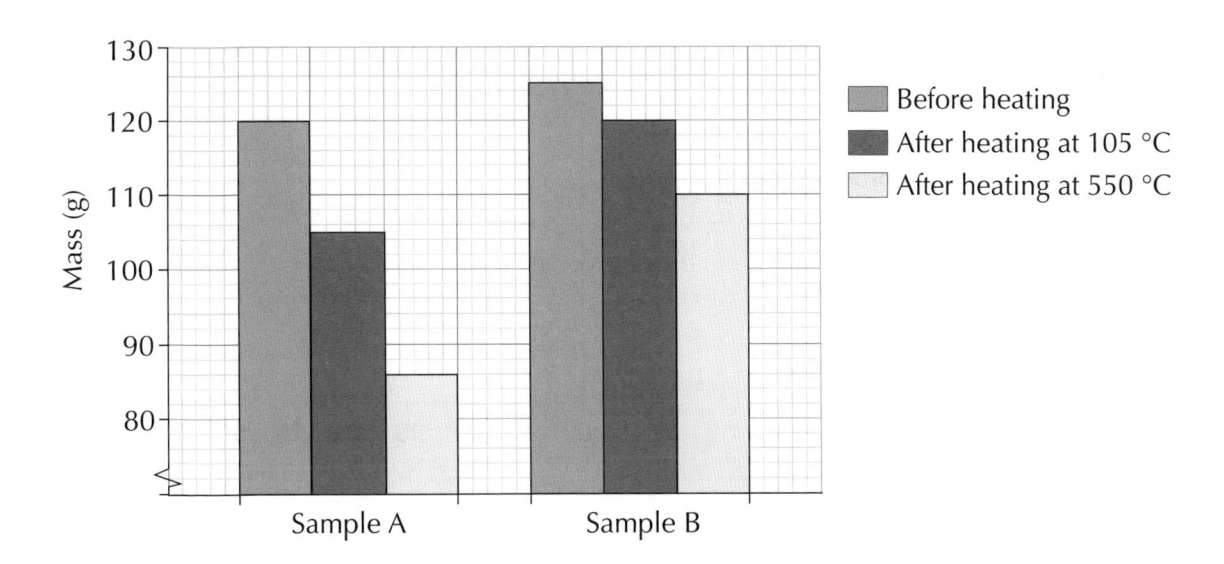

BIOLOGY

Q4 Josh is plotting a bar graph of the energy sources a country uses to generate electricity. What percentage should his bar for 'nuclear' be worth?

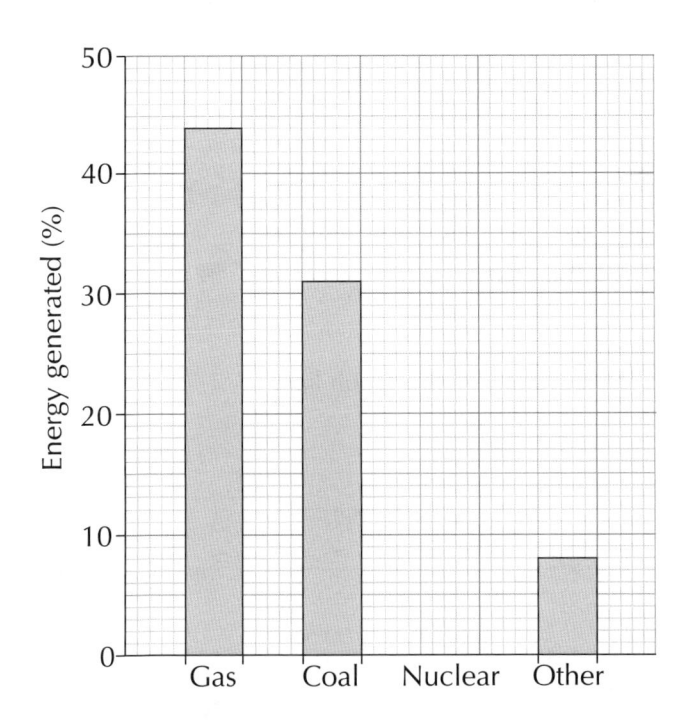

PHYSICS

Section 3 — Analysing Data

Interpreting Line Graphs

Line graphs can show how a variable changes over time. So as well as being asked to read a value from a graph, or do a calculation using numbers you've plucked from it, you might be asked to describe the trend it shows over time. Sounds like it's worth getting a bit of practice in doing just that, so read on...

Example

Martin carried out a chemical reaction and recorded how much product was formed over time. He plotted his results on the line graph opposite.

a) How much product had formed after 12 seconds?

b) Describe the trend in the data.

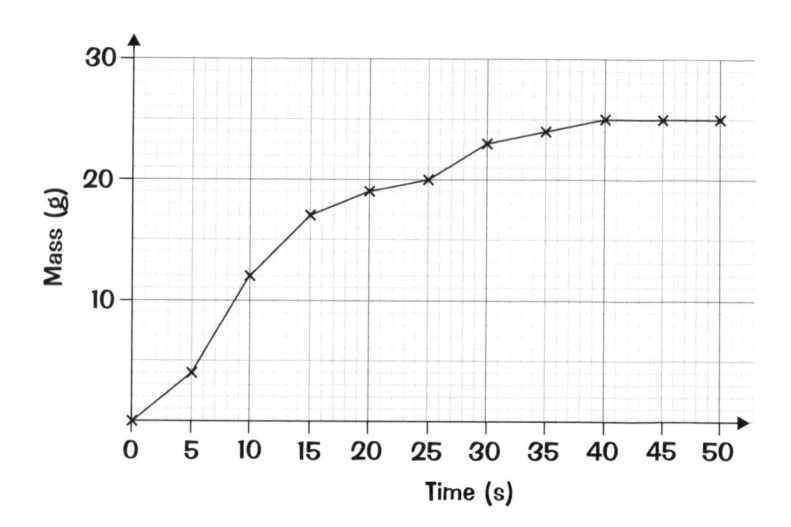

First, focus on part a)...

1 Find the axis that contains the value mentioned in the question.

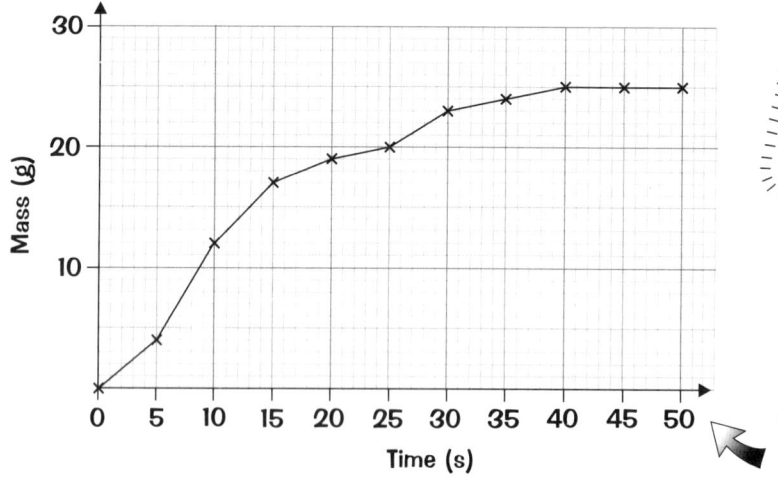

Usually, the independent variable (the thing that was changed) goes along x-axis. The dependent variable (the thing that was measured) goes up the y-axis.

The question specifies the time, so you need to start by looking at the x-axis.

2 Draw a line up from the value in the question to the graph line.

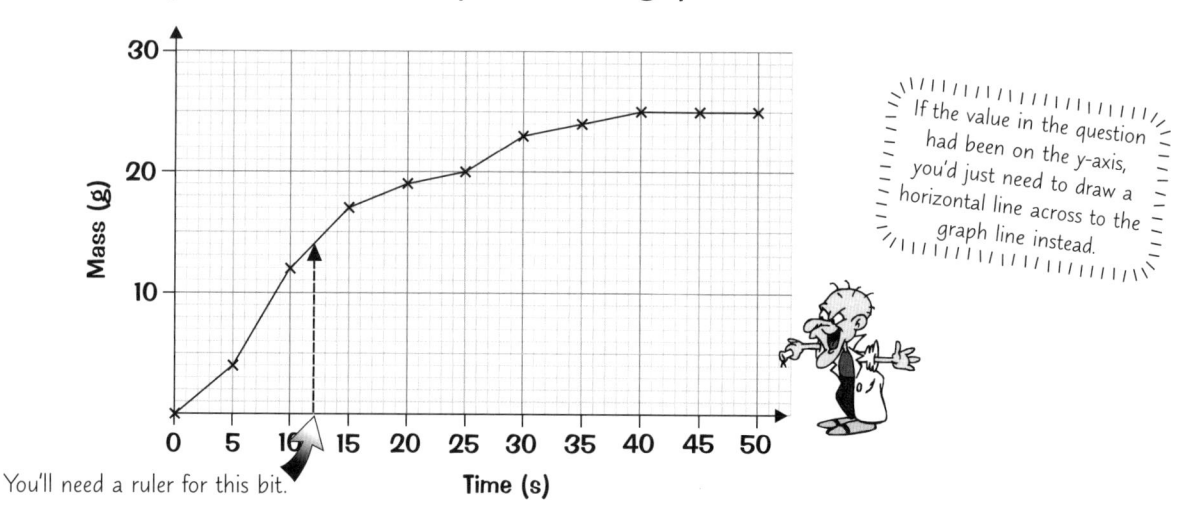

If the value in the question had been on the y-axis, you'd just need to draw a horizontal line across to the graph line instead.

You'll need a ruler for this bit.

Section 3 — Analysing Data

3 Draw a line across from this point to the opposite axis.

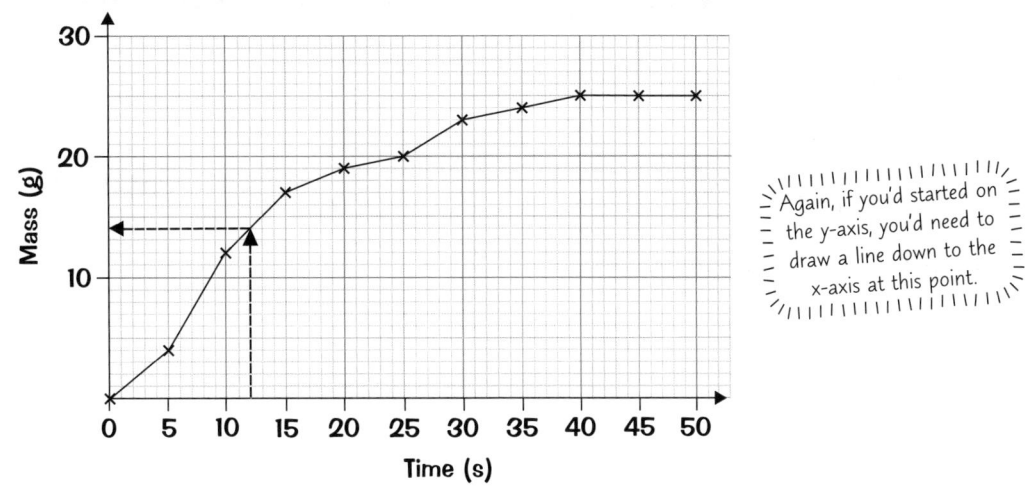

Again, if you'd started on the y-axis, you'd need to draw a line down to the x-axis at this point.

4 Read off the value from that axis.

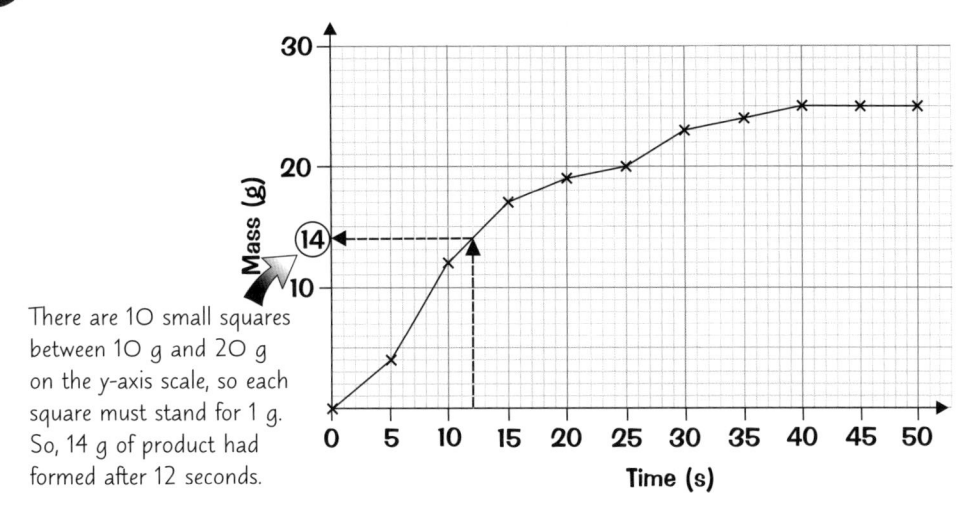

There are 10 small squares between 10 g and 20 g on the y-axis scale, so each square must stand for 1 g. So, 14 g of product had formed after 12 seconds.

Now for part b)...

1 Look for any patterns in the data...

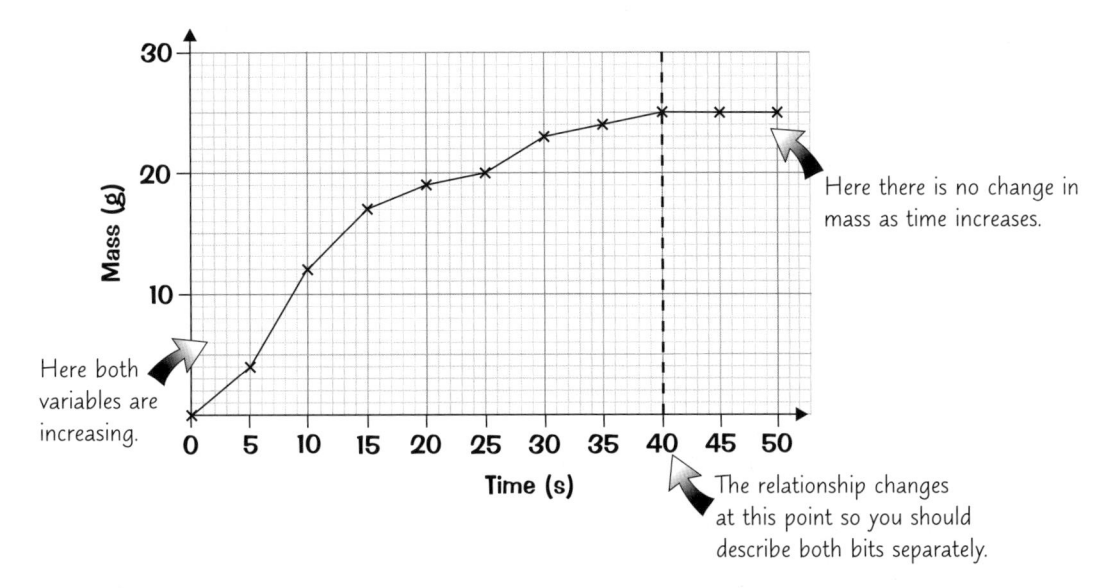

Here both variables are increasing.

Here there is no change in mass as time increases.

The relationship changes at this point so you should describe both bits separately.

2 ... and then put them into words. It's useful to add in relevant values in your description.

'For the first 40 seconds the mass of product increases, but it levels off after this and doesn't increase any further.'

Section 3 — Analysing Data

Interpreting Line Graphs

If you're having any doubts about line graphs, there's more practice here than you can shake a stick at.

Q1 Yasir measured the activity of a radioactive material over several hours and plotted his results on the graph below. **PHYSICS**

   a) Describe the trend in the data.

   b) What was the count rate after three minutes?

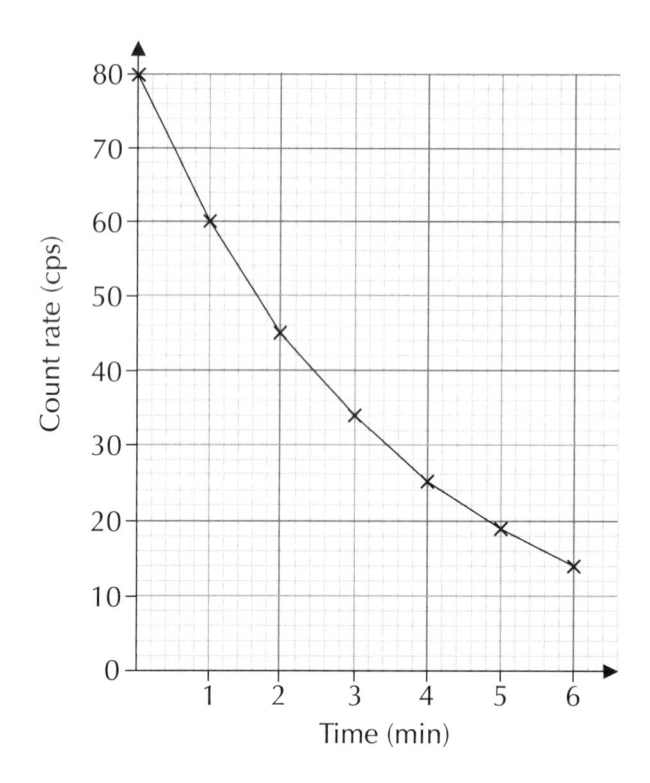

Q2 In 1970, a new antibiotic was discovered which was effective against disease X. The graph shows the number of deaths from disease X in the years since 1970. How many more deaths from disease X were there in 1970 than in 2000? **BIOLOGY**

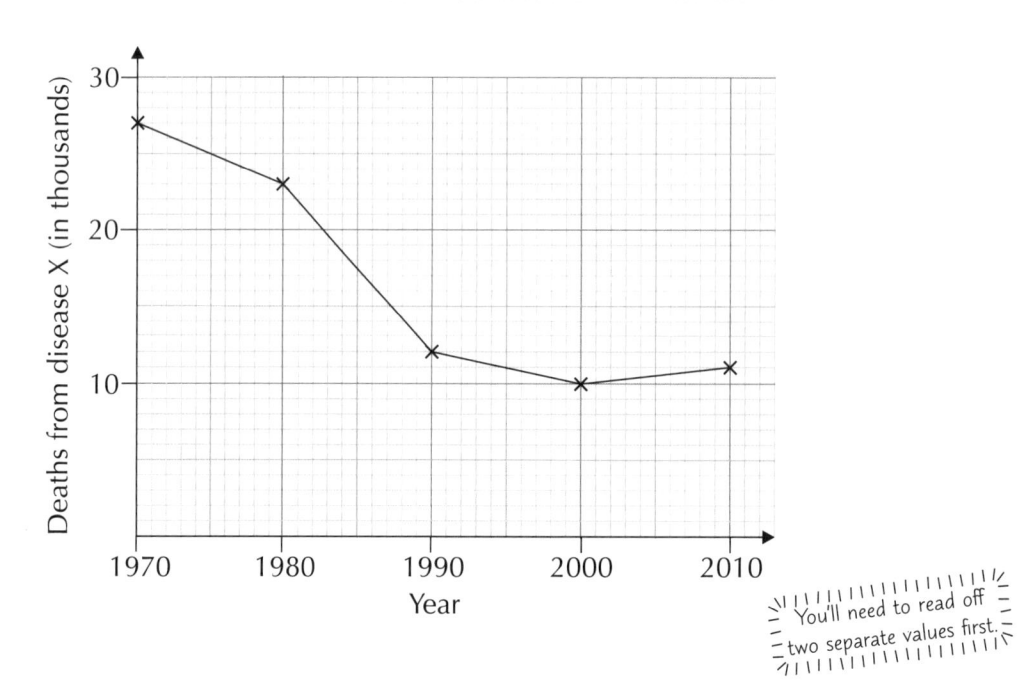

You'll need to read off two separate values first.

Section 3 — Analysing Data

Q3 A student measured the amount of hydrogen gas produced by a chemical reaction. The results are shown in the line graph below. **CHEMISTRY**

  a) How much gas was produced after 15 seconds?

  b) Describe the trend in the data.

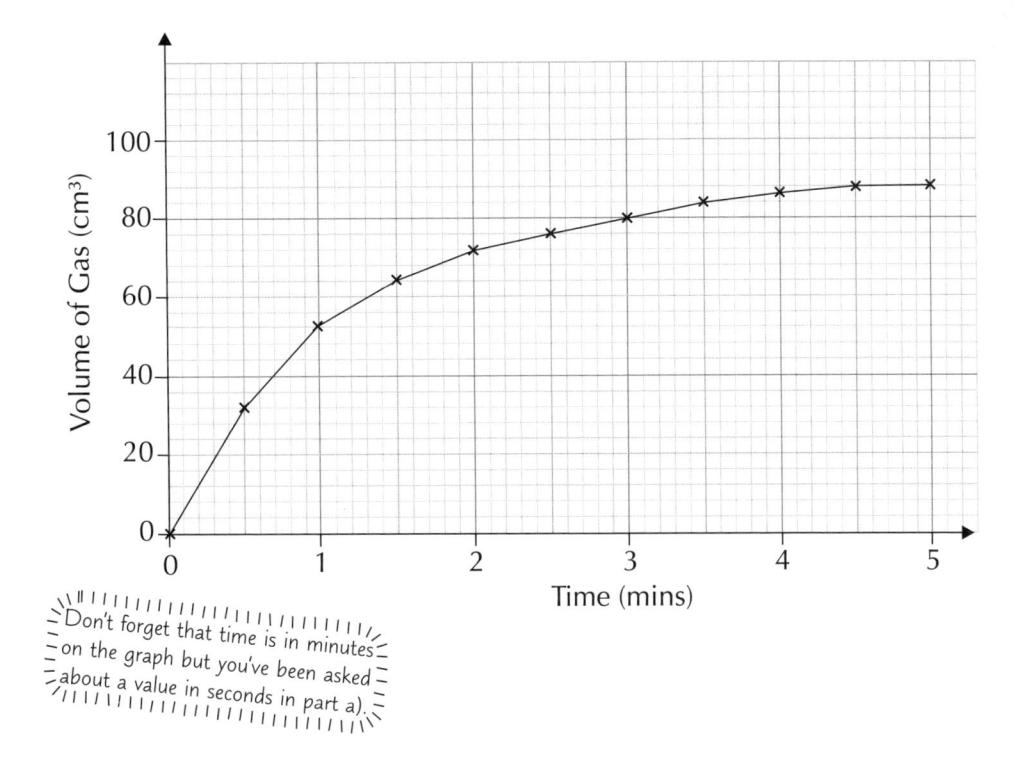

Don't forget that time is in minutes on the graph but you've been asked about a value in seconds in part a).

Q4 Susan was investigating the effect of exercise on breathing rate. She recorded her breathing rate every 30 seconds, starting from one minute before going for a short sprint. **BIOLOGY**

  a) By how much did Susan's breathing rate increase during her study?

  b) From its highest point, how long did it take Susan's breathing rate to return back to its starting rate?

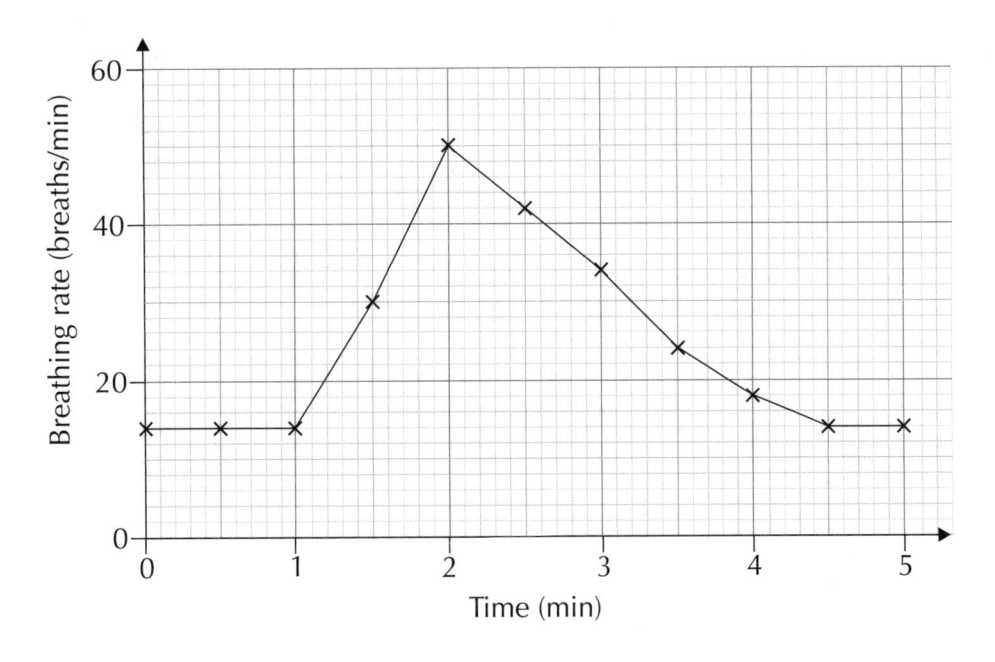

Section 3 — Analysing Data

Interpreting Scatter Graphs

Scatter graphs are really good at showing the relationship between two variables. And the fun doesn't stop there — you can even describe that relationship with fancy words like correlation and directly proportional. I bet you can't wait to get stuck in — it's a page of graphical treats.

Example

Simon did an experiment to investigate how temperature affects the rate of a reaction, and plotted a graph of his results. What type of correlation does the graph show?

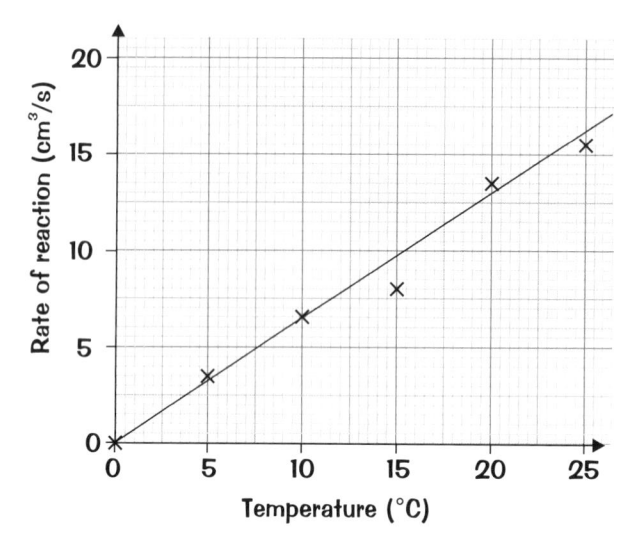

A correlation is a relationship between two variables.

1) Look at the direction of the line of best fit.
There are two types of correlation it could look like (or if you couldn't draw a line of best fit, there's probably no correlation at all).

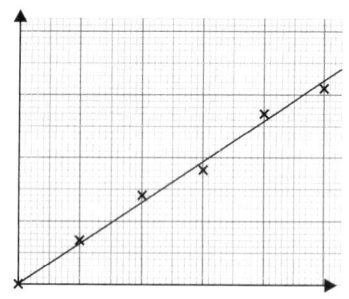

If both values increase together, it's known as a positive correlation.

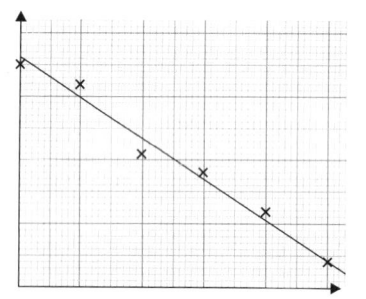

It's called a negative correlation if one value increases as the other decreases.

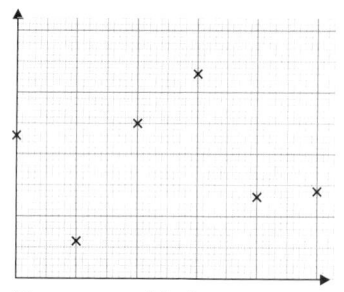

If one variable has no effect on the other, there's no correlation at all. There's no hope of drawing a line of best fit here.

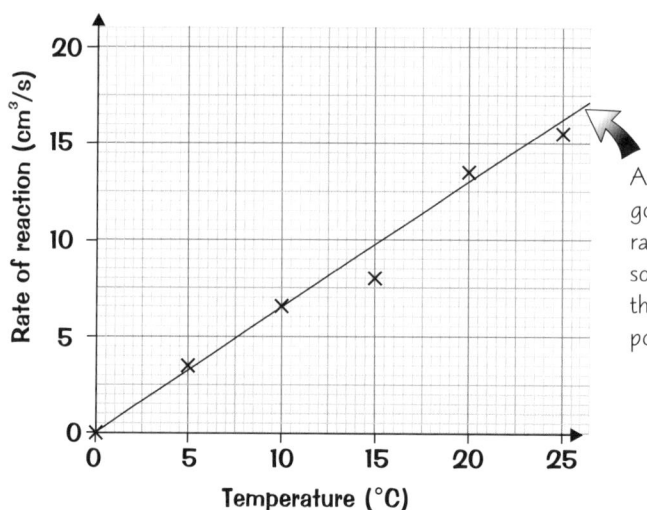

As the temperature goes up, so does the rate of reaction — so you can say that the graph shows a positive correlation.

Section 3 — Analysing Data

2) Once you've found a correlation, look to see whether it's a proportional relationship. This is where both variables increase (or decrease) at the same rate. There are two types you could look for:

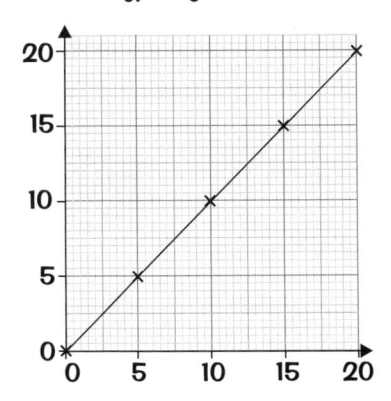

Both values increase at the same rate (e.g. as one thing doubles, the other thing also doubles) — this is a directly proportional relationship. A trick to spotting these is if the graph is a straight line that passes through the origin (0,0).

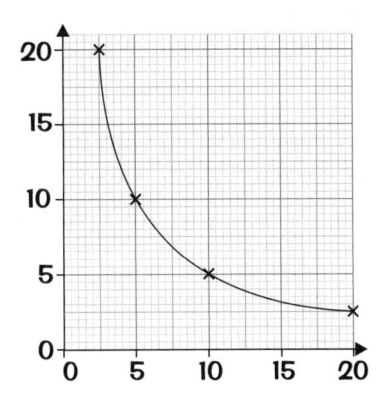

As one value increases, the other decreases at the same rate (e.g. as one thing doubles, the other thing halves) — this is an indirectly proportional (or inversely proportional) relationship.

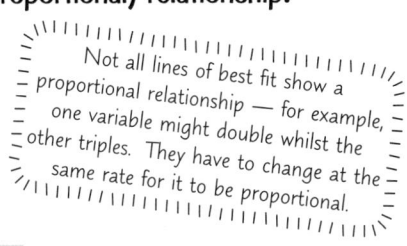

Not all lines of best fit show a proportional relationship — for example, one variable might double whilst the other triples. They have to change at the same rate for it to be proportional.

Back to the graph in the question now...

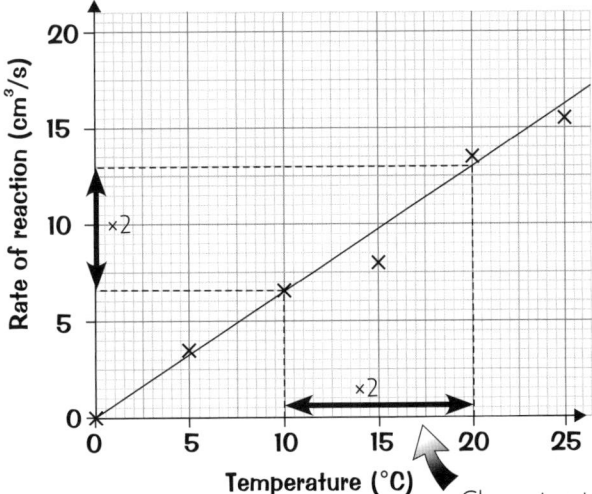

Any graph where the line of best fit is a straight line (rather than a curve) can be said to show a linear relationship.

Choose two temperatures, one which is double the other, e.g. 10 °C and 20 °C. Look at what the rate of reaction is at these two temperatures.

At 10 °C, the rate is 6.5 cm³/s
At 20 °C, the rate is 13 cm³/s.

13 ÷ 6.5 = 2, so the rate is doubled as well.

So you can say that the rate of reaction is directly proportional to the temperature.

3) Here's another good use for lines and crosses.

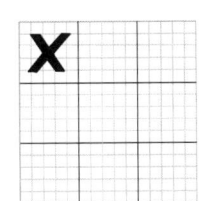

Your move.

Section 3 — Analysing Data

Interpreting Scatter Graphs

The ups and downs of relationships — it's exciting stuff. Here are some lovely scatter graphs complete with lines of best fit so you can put your new-found relationship knowledge to the test.

Q1 A gas syringe was filled with increasing volumes of a gas at a constant temperature and the pressure inside the syringe was measured. Describe the relationship shown by the graph below.

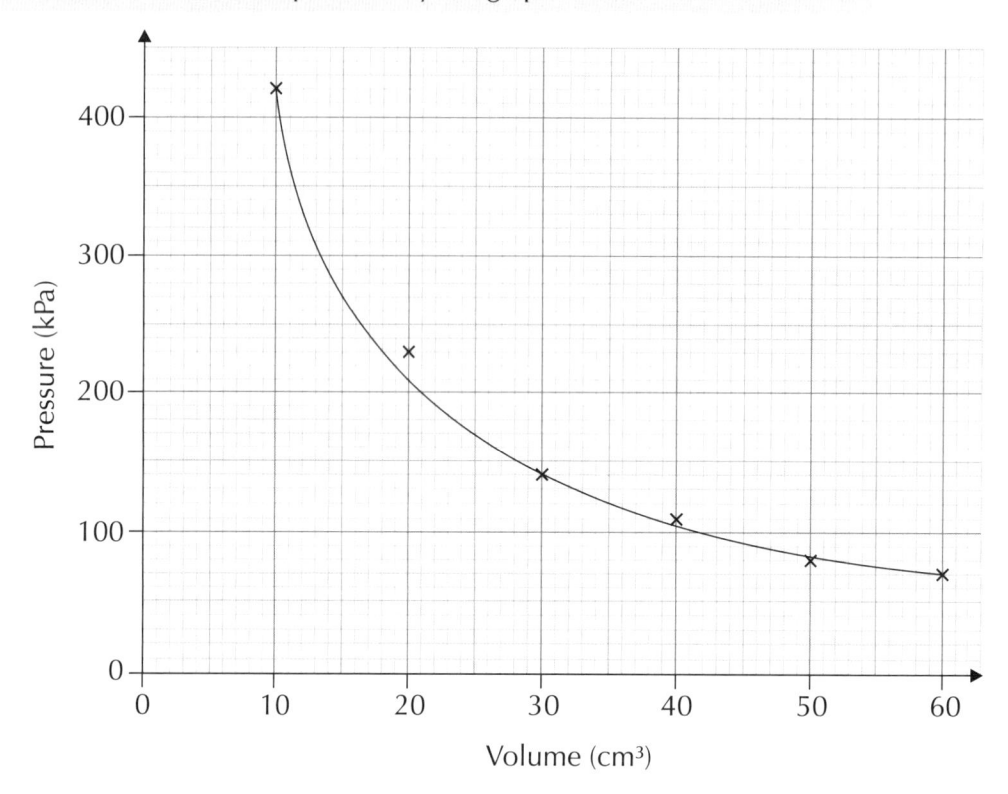

PHYSICS

Q2 Some students did an experiment to find out how increasing the concentration of acid affects the amount of heat produced in a neutralisation reaction. Describe the trend in their results.

CHEMISTRY

A relationship might also be referred to as a trend.

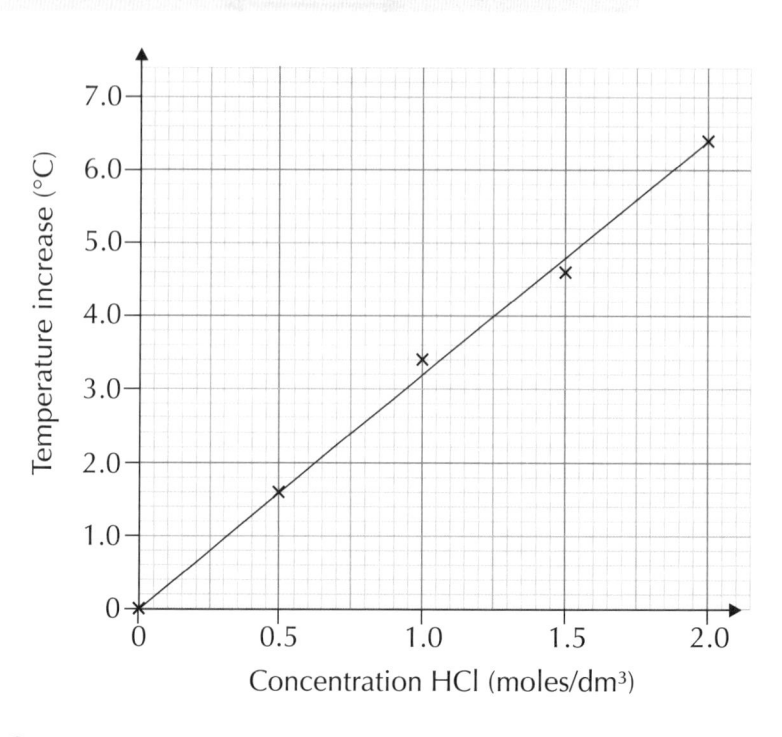

Section 3 — Analysing Data

Q3 The graph below show the results of study investigating the link between the number of bees in an area and the temperature of the area. Describe the relationship it shows.

BIOLOGY

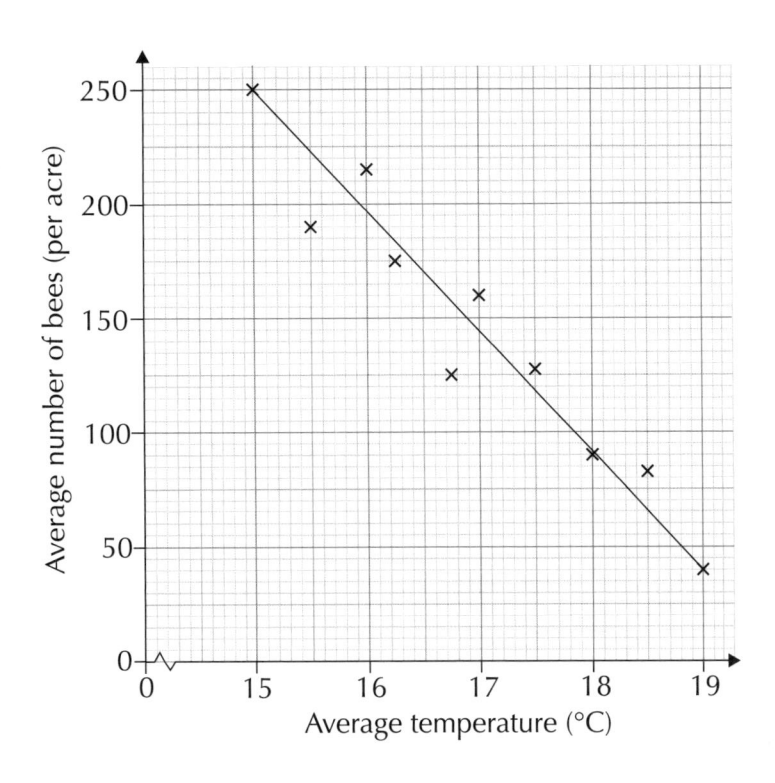

Average number of bees (per acre) vs *Average temperature (°C)*

Q4 Chris investigated the effect of different voltages on the current in a circuit. His results are shown below. Describe the relationship shown by the graph.

PHYSICS

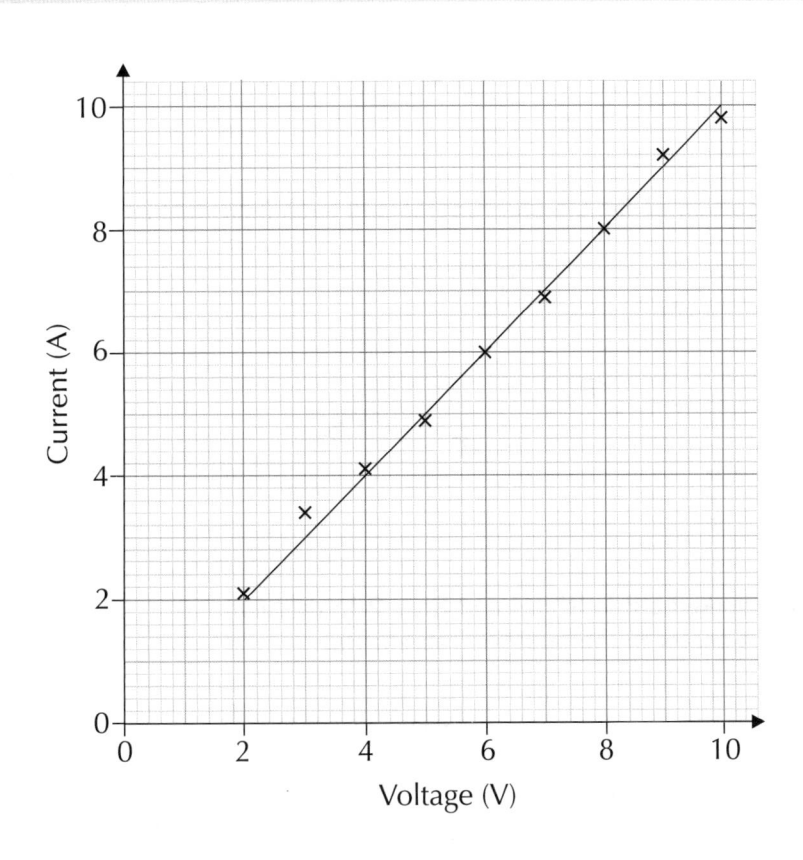

Current (A) vs *Voltage (V)*

Section 3 — Analysing Data

Interpreting Pie Charts

Pie charts are divided into sectors that represent categories — the size of each sector tells you how much of the total data is in that category. Think of data like a hot apple filling. Mmmm...

Example

Lucy did a survey to find out how much exercise people do in a week. She asked 30 people and drew a pie chart of her results.

How many of the people exercise for less than 1 hour per week?

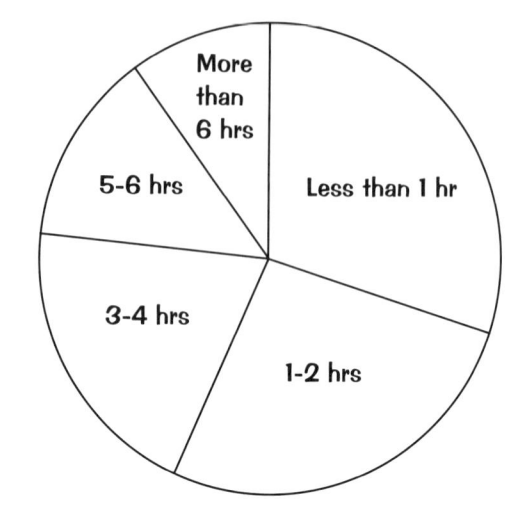

1) Measure the angle of the sector you're interested in.

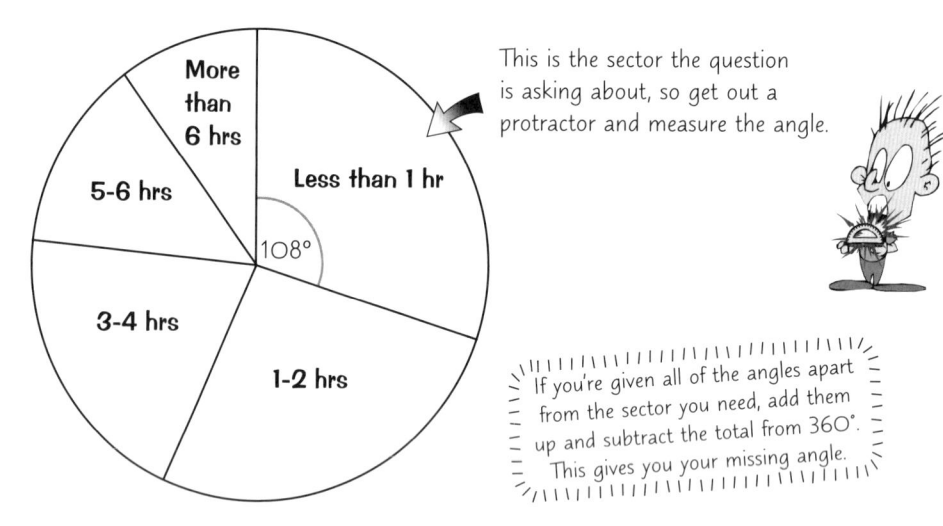

This is the sector the question is asking about, so get out a protractor and measure the angle.

If you're given all of the angles apart from the sector you need, add them up and subtract the total from 360°. This gives you your missing angle.

2) Calculate what proportion of the pie chart represents each individual person.

The whole pie chart (all 360°) represents 30 people, so you need to find out how many degrees represents one person...

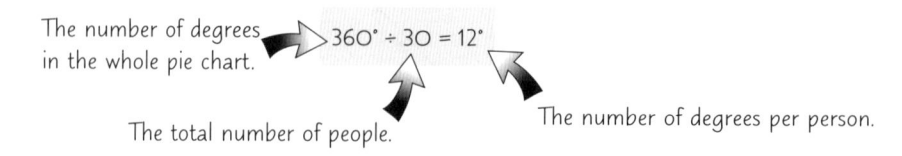

The number of degrees in the whole pie chart. → 360° ÷ 30 = 12°

The total number of people. The number of degrees per person.

3) Use the values you worked out in Step 1 and Step 2 to calculate how many people the sector in the question represents.

108° ÷ 12° = 9

The size of the sector in the pie chart.

The number of degrees each person is represented by.

The number of people in that category. Phew.

Section 3 — Analysing Data

Interpreting Pie Charts

All it takes is some practice, then getting data from a pie chart will be as easy as... well, pie.

Q1 The pie chart below shows the relative amounts of ionising radiation from its different sources that residents are exposed to in one town. What percentage of the radiation comes from food? **PHYSICS**

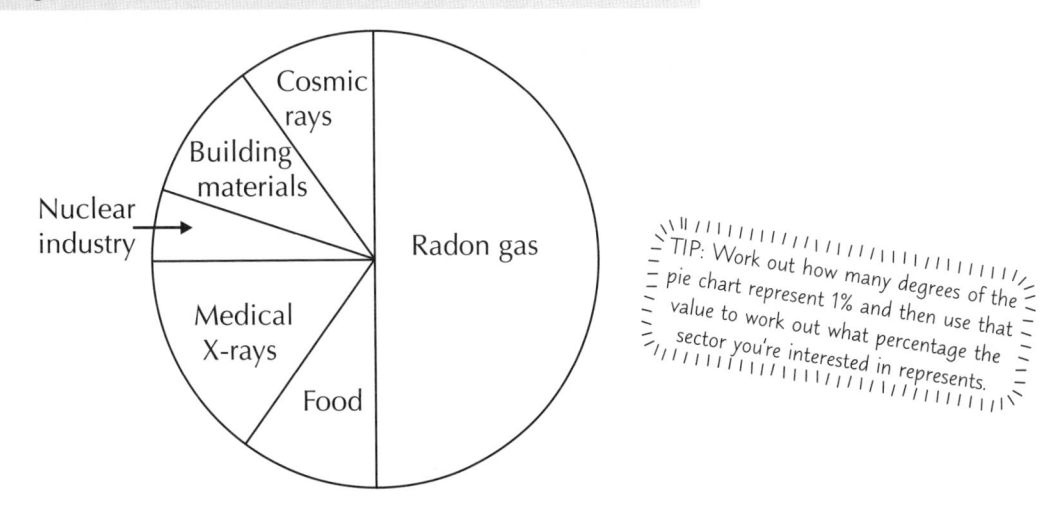

TIP: Work out how many degrees of the pie chart represent 1% and then use that value to work out what percentage the sector you're interested in represents.

Q2 The proportions of the elements in ethanol are shown in this pie chart. How many grams of hydrogen are in 46 g of ethanol? **CHEMISTRY**

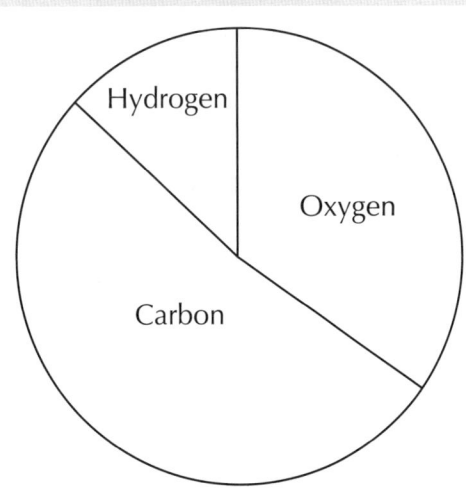

Q3 Gemma investigated the nutritional contents of one type of food. The food sample had a total mass of 40 g. How many grams of protein were there? **BIOLOGY**

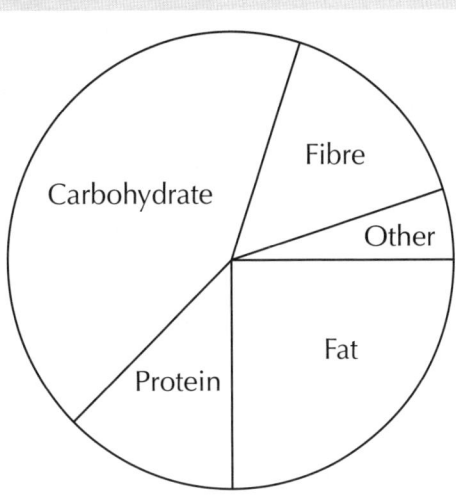

Section 3 — Analysing Data

Interpreting Histograms

Histograms are kind of like bar charts, but it's the area of the bar that's important rather than the height. That means a bit of calculating is involved to wrestle the data out of them. Calculator at the ready...

Example

Martin was investigating the boiling points of a range of substances. His results are in this histogram.

How many substances had a boiling point between 100 °C and 110 °C?

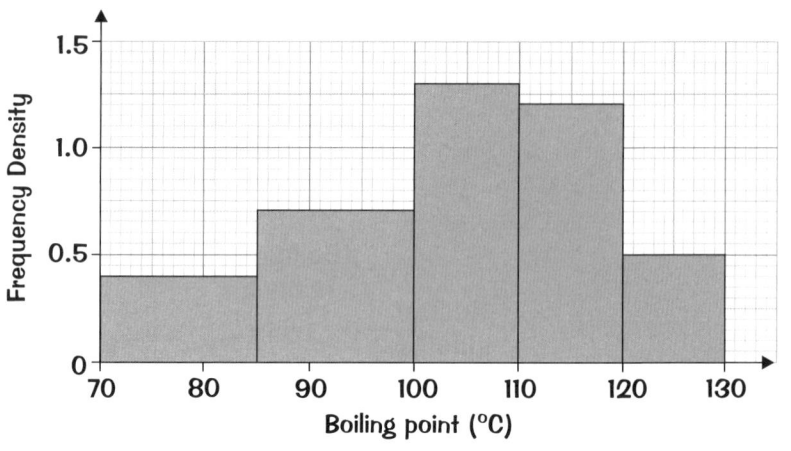

1 Pick the class (or classes) you need to look at.

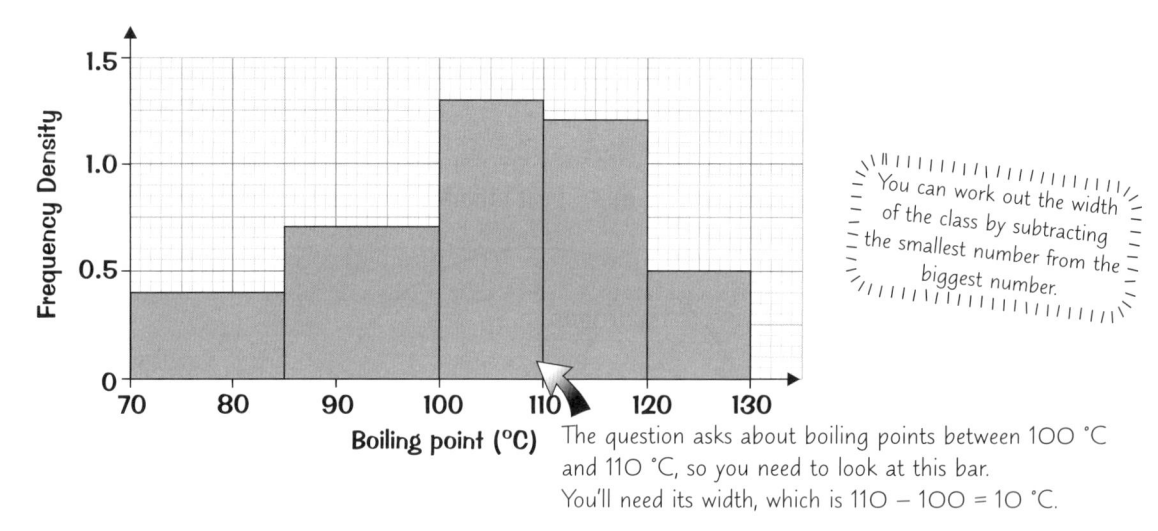

You can work out the width of the class by subtracting the smallest number from the biggest number.

The question asks about boiling points between 100 °C and 110 °C, so you need to look at this bar. You'll need its width, which is 110 − 100 = 10 °C.

2 Read across from the height of the bar to the number on the y-axis.

There are 10 small squares between 1.0 and 1.5, so each square must stand for 0.05. Reading across, the top of the bar is at 1.3.

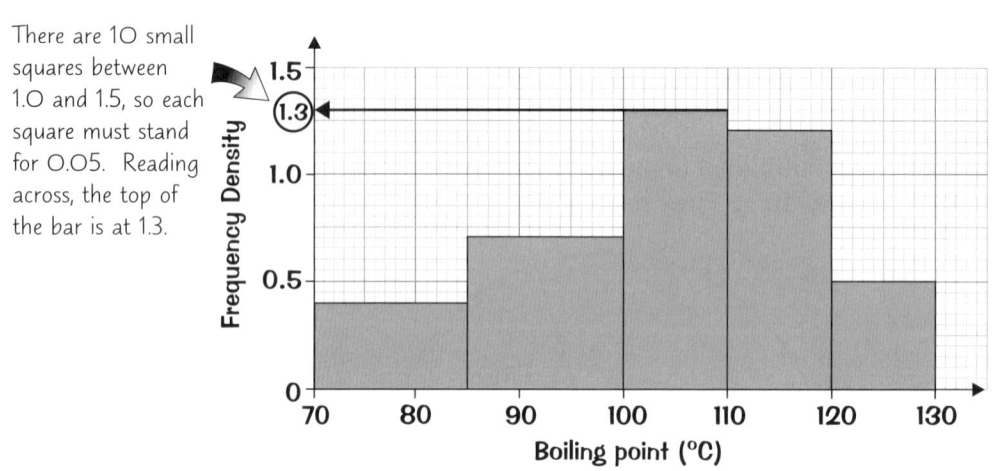

3 Multiply the width of the bar (the class width) by the height of the bar (the frequency density).

10 × 1.3 = 13

Class width
Frequency density

Frequency — this is the number of substances in this class. So 13 substances had a boiling point between 100 and 110 °C.

Section 3 — Analysing Data

Interpreting Histograms

It's time to let these histograms know who's boss. Grab your calculator and have a go at these questions...

Q1 A selection of metal items were tested as resistors in an electric circuit. A histogram of their resistances is shown below. How many of the items tested had resistance between 5 Ω and 10 Ω? **PHYSICS**

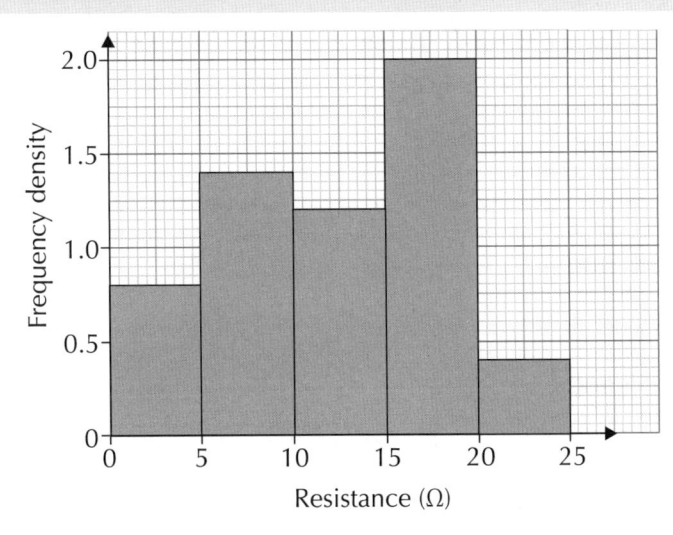

Q2 Sandra was investigating the range of heights of students in her class. She made a histogram of her results. How many students are less than 150 cm tall? **BIOLOGY**

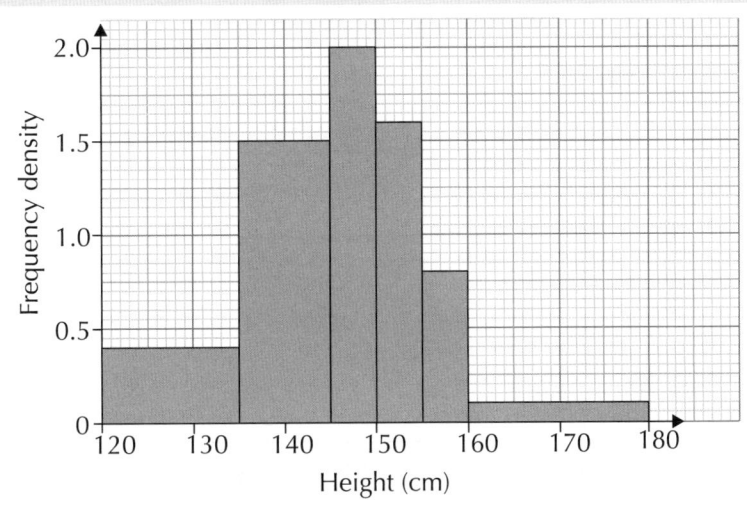

TIP: Work out the frequency for each class separately, then add them together to get the total number of students.

Q3 The histogram below shows the energy output for different samples of fuel. How many samples have an energy output of more than 20 J/g? **CHEMISTRY**

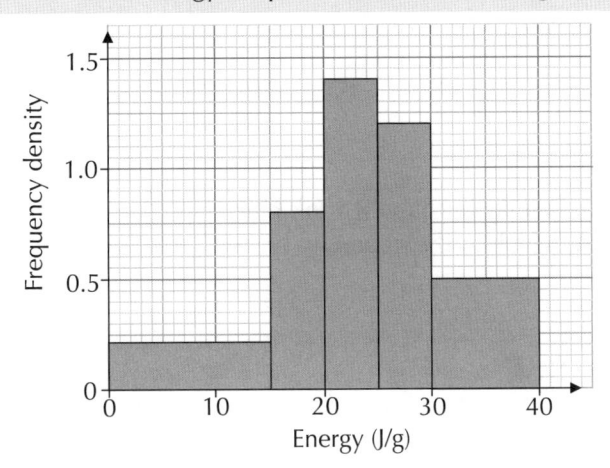

Section 3 — Analysing Data

Distance-Time Graphs — Calculating Speed

Distance-time graphs show you exactly that — distance travelled and time taken. The gradient (the slope) of a distance-time graph is equal to the speed the object is going. Pretty nifty if you ask me.

Example

Joe was driving home along a straight road. Below is a distance-time graph of the start of his journey. Calculate the speed he was travelling at between 15 and 40 seconds.

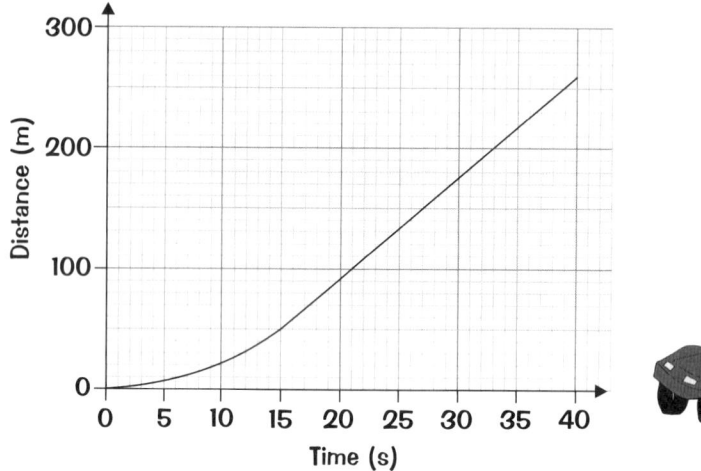

1 Work out the distance he travelled between 15 and 40 seconds.

Distance is measured up the y-axis. The distance Joe travelled between 15 and 40 seconds is:

260 − 50 = 210 metres

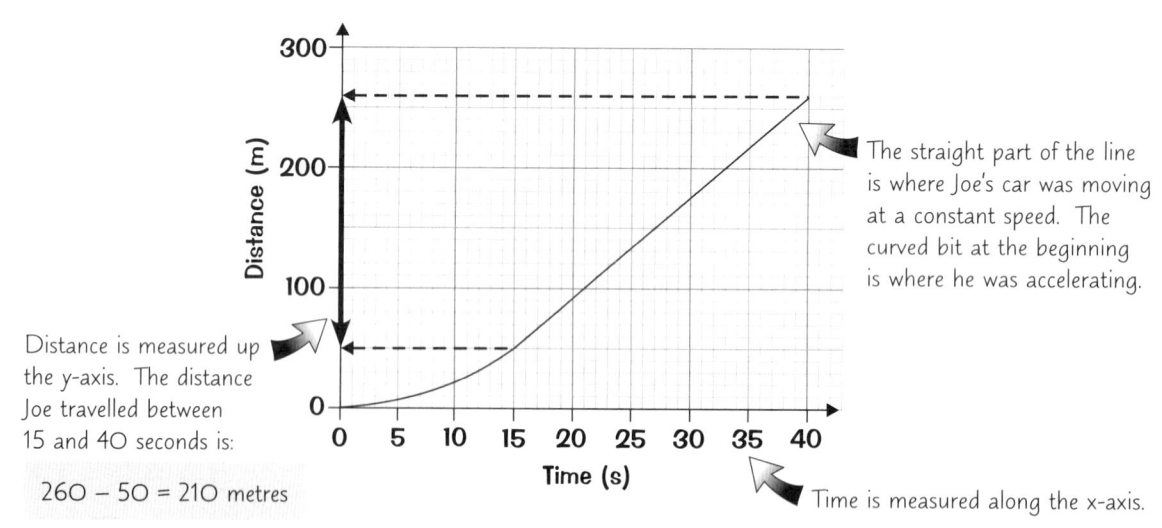

The straight part of the line is where Joe's car was moving at a constant speed. The curved bit at the beginning is where he was accelerating.

Time is measured along the x-axis.

2 Work out the time taken.

You're given the numbers in the question, so:

40 seconds − 15 seconds = 25 seconds

3 Divide the distance he travelled by the time it took him. This gives you the gradient, which is the speed.

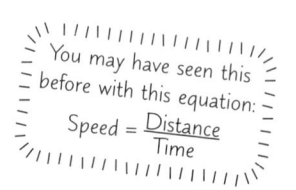

210 m ÷ 25 s = 8.4 m/s

The distance travelled. The time taken. This is his speed.
The units are m/s because the distance was measured in metres and the time was measured in seconds.

You may have seen this before with this equation:

$$\text{Speed} = \frac{\text{Distance}}{\text{Time}}$$

Section 3 — Analysing Data

Distance-Time Graphs — Calculating Speed

Being able to calculate a gradient is pretty important with these graphs. See how you get on with this lot...

Q1 Rajni walked the length of a road. She rested for two minutes then jogged back to her start point, as shown in the graph below. **PHYSICS**

a) What was her speed as she walked to the end of the road?

b) At what speed did she jog back to the start point?

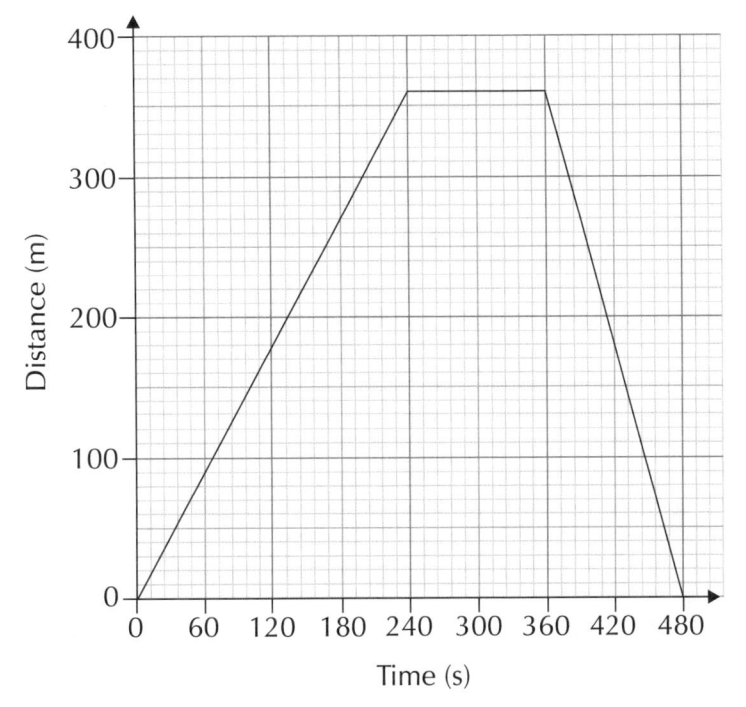

Flat sections of the graph are where there's no movement. Downhill sections are where the person or object is returning to the starting point.

Q2 The distance-time graph below shows the distance a bus travelled from its starting point plotted against time. What was its speed between 30 and 50 seconds? **PHYSICS**

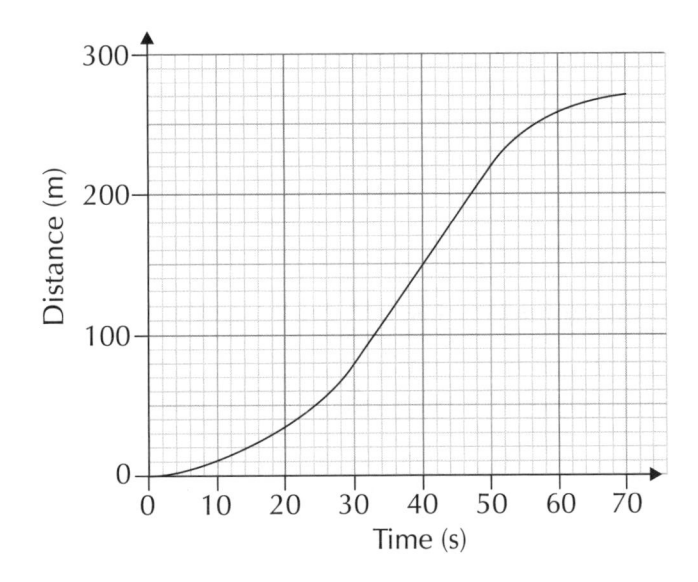

Section 3 — Analysing Data

Velocity-Time Graphs — Calculating Acceleration

Velocity is speed with a direction. When it's plotted against time on a graph, you can use it to calculate the acceleration of an object, since the acceleration is equal to the gradient of the line. And here's how...

Example

On the right is a velocity-time graph of a car travelling along a straight road.

What is its acceleration between 10 and 20 seconds?

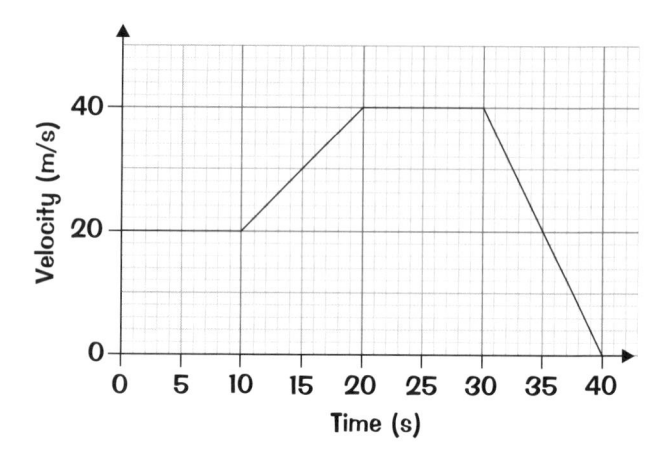

1 Work out the change in velocity by subtracting the initial velocity from the final velocity.

Velocity is measured on the y-axis, so subtract the initial velocity from the final velocity:

40 − 20 = 20 m/s

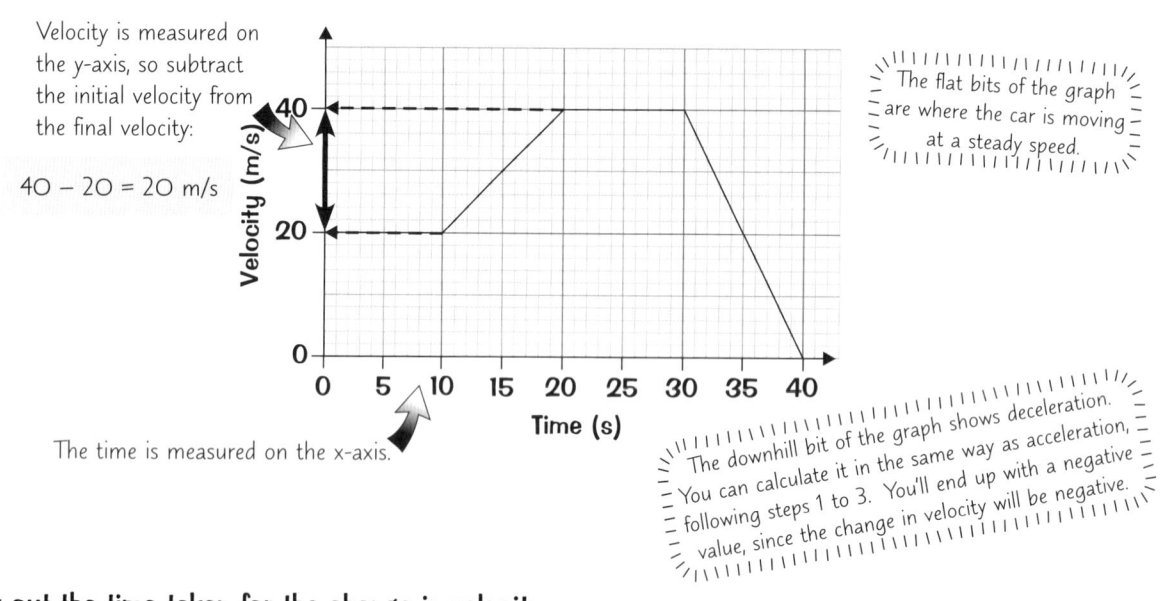

The time is measured on the x-axis.

The flat bits of the graph are where the car is moving at a steady speed.

The downhill bit of the graph shows deceleration. You can calculate it in the same way as acceleration, following steps 1 to 3. You'll end up with a negative value, since the change in velocity will be negative.

2 Work out the time taken for the change in velocity.

You've been given the numbers you need in the question, so:

20 seconds − 10 seconds = 10 seconds

3 Divide the change in velocity by the time taken to get the gradient — that's the acceleration.

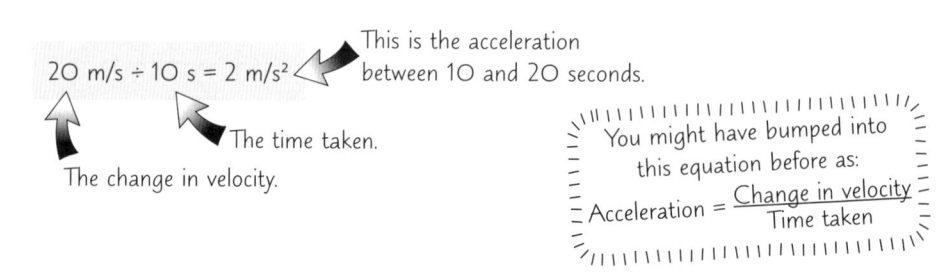

20 m/s ÷ 10 s = 2 m/s²

This is the acceleration between 10 and 20 seconds.

The change in velocity. The time taken.

You might have bumped into this equation before as:

$$\text{Acceleration} = \frac{\text{Change in velocity}}{\text{Time taken}}$$

Section 3 — Analysing Data

Velocity-Time Graphs — Calculating Acceleration

Learning how to calculate gradients can be a bit of an uphill struggle. But never fear — here are some lovely velocity-time graphs for you to put that learning into practice.

Q1 The graph below shows the velocity of a cyclist plotted against time. What is the cyclist's acceleration between 2 and 5 seconds?

PHYSICS

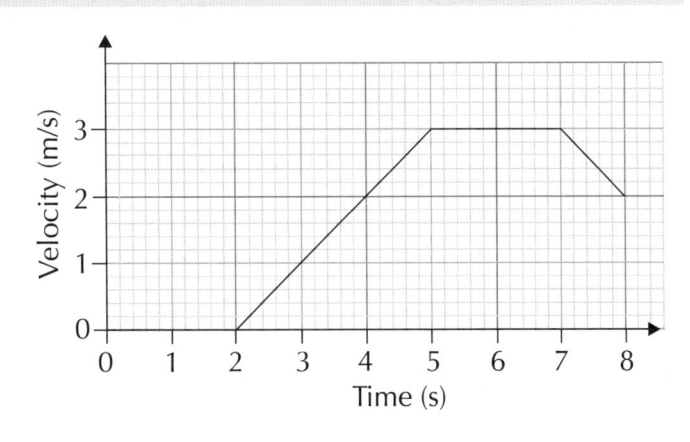

Q2 A race car accelerates to 50 m/s. Calculate its acceleration between 3 and 6 seconds from the velocity-time graph below.

PHYSICS

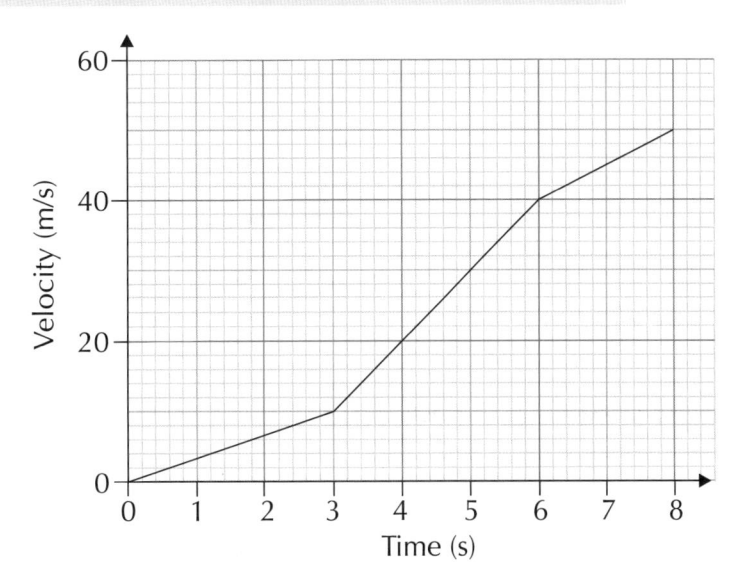

Q3 A ball rolls across a flat surface until it comes to a stop. What is its deceleration?

PHYSICS

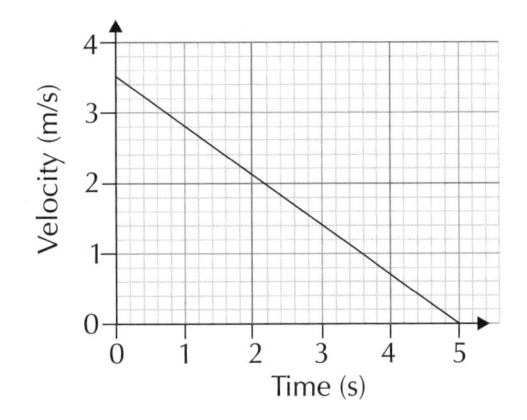

Remember, to find the change in velocity you subtract the initial velocity from the final velocity.

Section 3 — Analysing Data

Velocity-Time Graphs — Calculating Distance

Velocity-time graphs can also be used to calculate the distance an object travels in a given time. No gradients needed this time — now it's all about the area underneath the graph.

Example

On the right is a velocity-time graph of a car travelling along a straight road.

What is the total distance it travelled between 20 and 30 seconds?

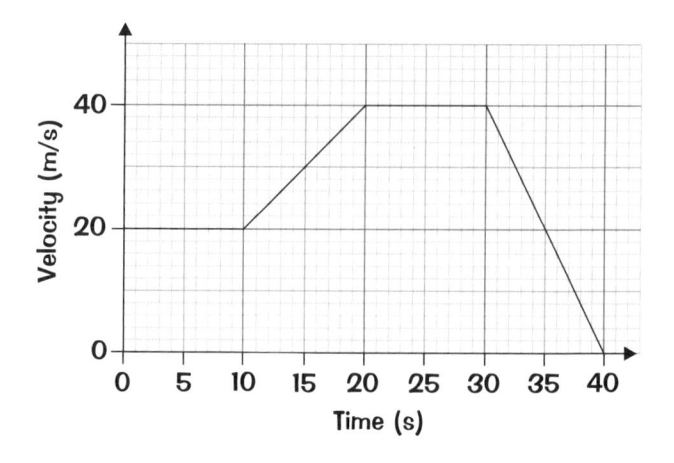

1) You need to work out the area under the graph for the time period mentioned in the question. So first, work out the width of the bit you're interested in.

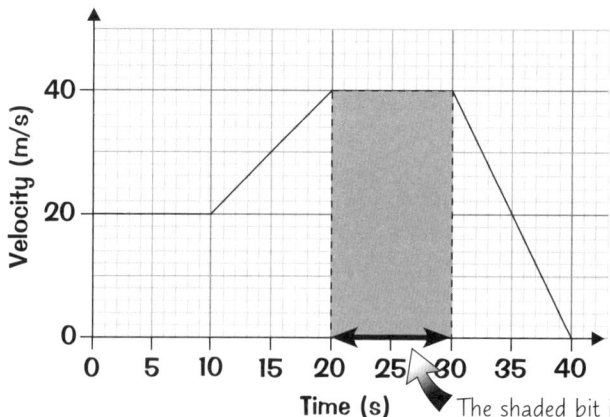

The shaded bit is the area you want to calculate. You can work out its width by subtracting the smaller x-axis value from the larger value.

$$30 - 20 = 10 \text{ s}$$

2) Next, work out the height of the bit you're interested in.

You can work out the height of the shaded area by reading it from the y-axis. Easy. Here it's 40 m/s.

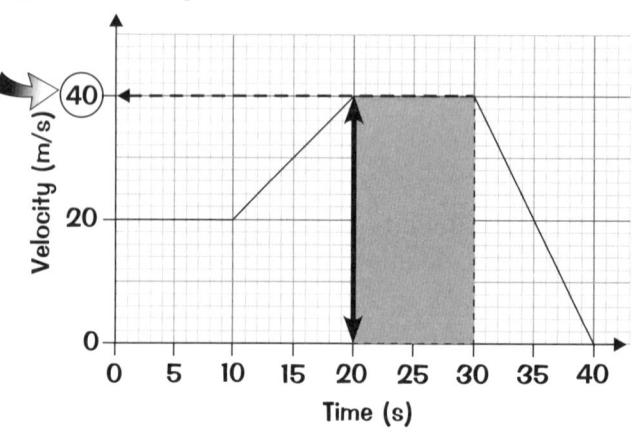

3) Multiply the width by the height to get the area — which gives you the distance travelled.

$$10 \text{ s} \times 40 \text{ m/s} = 400 \text{ m}$$

This is the distance travelled between 20 and 30 seconds.

Section 3 — Analysing Data

Velocity-Time Graphs — Calculating Distance

It's your turn now. Have a go at working out the distances from this whole new bunch of velocity-time graphs.

Q1 The graph below shows the velocity of a cyclist plotted against time. How far did the cyclist travel between 2 and 5 seconds?

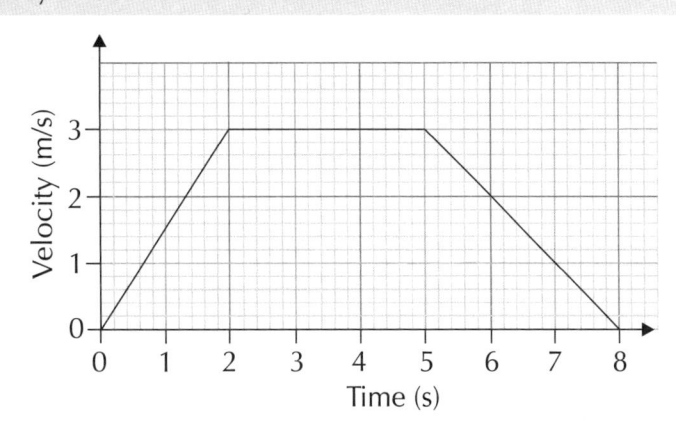

Q2 The graph below shows the velocity of a skydiver after he jumps out of a plane. After 40 seconds he opens his parachute — how far does he fall before then?

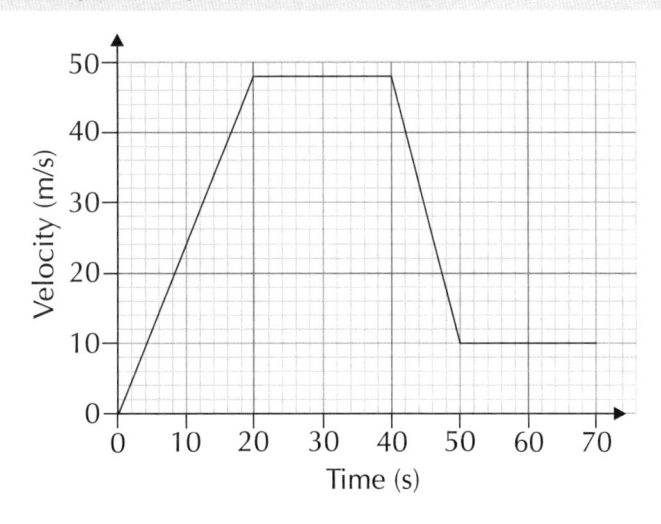

TIP: It'll be easier here if you split the area into two shapes. The area of a triangle is given by ½ × base × height.

Q3 Lisa is running in a race at a steady velocity. When she sees the finish line, she accelerates until she crosses it 5 seconds later. How far did she run between the start of her acceleration and crossing the finish line?

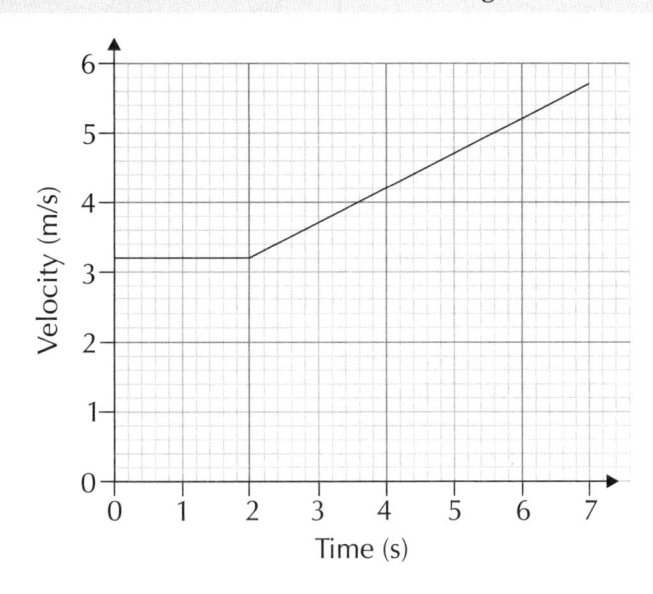

Section 3 — Analysing Data

Conclusions and Evaluations

Scientific investigations are finished off with a conclusion and evaluation. The conclusion is where you sum up what your data shows, while the evaluation takes apart the method and discusses what could be improved. It's time to be honest — 'the experiment was perfect' just won't cut it I'm afraid.

Example

Adil carried out an investigation to test this hypothesis:

Antibiotic X will be the most effective at killing bacteria.

His method was as follows:
- Grow one type of bacteria on some agar jelly in a Petri dish.
- Soak three paper discs each in a solution of a different antibiotic — X, Y or Z.
- Soak a fourth paper disc in water.
- Space the discs out on top of the agar.
- Keep the dish at 35 °C for two days.
- Measure the diameter of the clear zone around the discs.

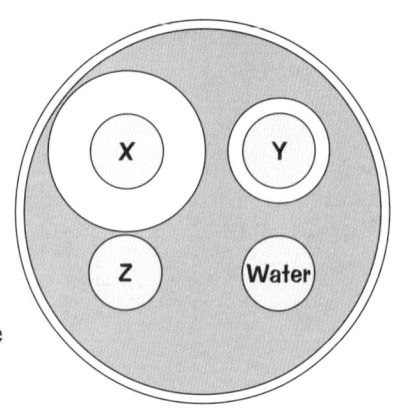

The table on the right shows his results.
Write a suitable conclusion and evaluation for this experiment.

Antibiotic	Clear zone (mm)
X	4
Y	2.5
Z	0
Water	0

1. Look at the data to see what it shows.

Antibiotic	Clear zone (mm)
X	4
Y	2.5
Z	0
Water	0

These are the antibiotics that were tested. So any conclusion can be about these three antibiotics only.

Antibiotic X had the largest clear zone, so it killed the most bacteria. However, you need to be careful that your conclusion doesn't go beyond the data. You can only conclude that antibiotic X is the most effective against the bacteria used in this experiment. Also, the results could be different if it was compared against other antibiotics.

Conclusion: Antibiotic X is more effective at killing this type of bacteria than antibiotics Y and Z.

2. Justify your conclusion using the results.

You could say something like:
After two days, the disc soaked in antibiotic X had a clear zone that had a diameter over 1½ times larger than the clear zone for antibiotic Y. Antibiotic Z had no apparent effect on the bacteria at all.

3. Look back to the hypothesis and say how well the conclusion supports it.

'Antibiotic X will be the most effective at killing bacteria.'

The conclusion supports this hypothesis as antibiotic X was the most effective out of those tested...

...but remember — you can't say if the hypothesis would still be true if different bacteria were used or if antibiotic X was compared against two new antibiotics. So although the conclusion provides some support for the hypothesis, it can't 100% prove it.

Section 3 — Analysing Data

So there you have your conclusion. Now on to evaluating the experiment...

1 Comment on the equipment and method used. Here are some questions you should consider:

- **Were the measurements taken carefully?** — This depends on the equipment used — if 25 cm³ of liquid was measured in a measuring cylinder with a scale divided into 10 cm³ sections, it's not likely to be an accurate amount. In this experiment, the amount of antibiotic used on each disc was not measured at all.

- **Were there any problems with the equipment?** — Equipment can break or it can be contaminated. For example, a different type of bacteria could have got into the Petri dish.

- **Was it difficult to measure or time anything?** — It might have been hard to measure the clear zone with a ruler if the zone was very small. This could lead to less accurate results.

- **Would repeating the experiment give the same results?** — It's entirely possible that the results occurred by chance. Adil did not repeat his experiment, so you don't know if his results are reliable or not.

- **Were there any anomalous results?** — This is more obvious if the experiment includes repeats. An anomalous result is a result that doesn't fit the pattern. If there is one, try to explain why — it's likely to be due to an inaccurate measurement or problems with the equipment.

- **Was a control used?** — A control is kept under the same conditions as the rest of the experiment, but doesn't have anything done to it. So Adil used water to show that the effects of the experiment were due to the antibiotics, and not due to the paper discs or anything else.

2 Suggest ways to improve the experiment and say why you would do them. You're looking for ways to make the results more accurate and reliable.

Reliable results can be repeated and reproduced by others. Accurate results are those that are really close to the true answer.

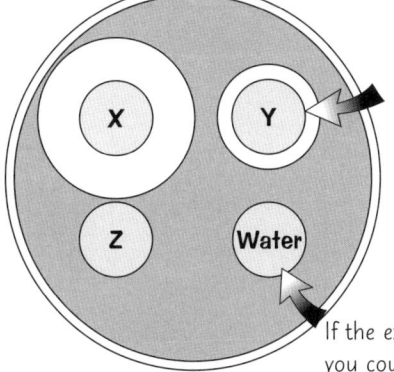

Instead of soaking the discs in antibiotic solution, you could pipette 1 ml of the antibiotic solution onto each of them. By using the same volume and concentration of antibiotic solution each time, you're making it a fair test and your results will be more reliable.

If the experiment did not have a control, you could add one.

Antibiotic	Clear zone (mm)
X	4
Y	2.5
Z	0
Water	0

You could repeat the experiment and calculate a mean value for each antibiotic to make the results more reliable. This will also help you to identify any anomalous results when you're processing your data.

3 Suggest ways to extend the experiment in order to find more support for the hypothesis.

The hypothesis was:

'Antibiotic X will be the most effective at killing bacteria.'

You could suggest a repeat of the investigation using a wider range of antibiotics to see if antibiotic X is still the most effective.

You could use different types of bacteria to see if antibiotic X is the most effective at killing other types of bacteria.

Section 3 — Analysing Data

Conclusions and Evaluations

Here's the moment you've been waiting for — the conclusion to this section. So here are some final questions for you. Get stuck into these and soon enough you'll be writing evaluations in your sleep.

Q1 Gemma was investigating the amount of energy released as heat when an acid reacts with a base. She hypothesised that 'increasing the concentration of acid will increase the amount of heat released by the reaction'.

CHEMISTRY

Her method was as follows:

- Measure 25 cm³ of sodium hydroxide solution in a beaker.
- Measure the temperature of the sodium hydroxide solution.
- Add 0.5 moles/dm³ hydrochloric acid.
- Measure the temperature again and record the temperature increase.
- Repeat with different concentrations of hydrochloric acid.
- Repeat the experiment two more times and calculate the average temperature increase for each concentration of acid.

Her results are shown below.

Concentration HCl (moles/dm³)	Temperature increase (°C)			
	Repeat 1	Repeat 2	Repeat 3	Average
0	0	0	0	0
0.5	1.5	1.8	1.5	1.6
1.0	3.3	3.8	3.4	3.5
1.5	2.7	4.4	4.2	4.3
2.0	6.1	6.5	6.6	6.4

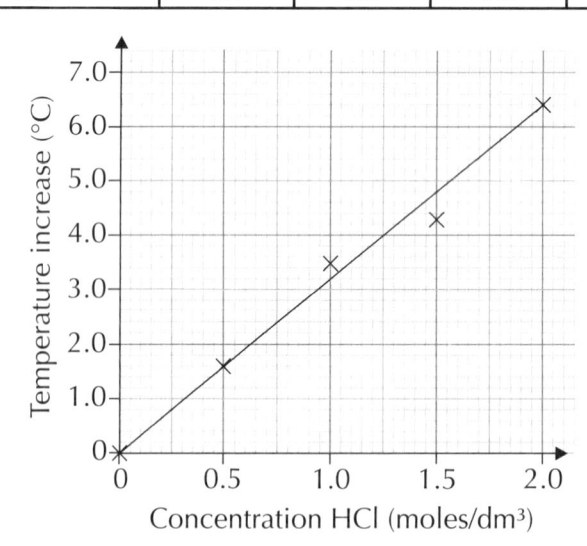

a) Write a suitable conclusion for this experiment.

b) Evaluate the experiment.

- Firstly, comment on the equipment and the method — think about the measurements, the apparatus, whether the experiment was repeated, if a control was used, etc.
- Then suggest some ways to improve the experiment, and say why they're better.
- Finally, come up with a possible extension to the investigation.

The evaluation isn't normally broken down like this, but I've done it just this once to give you a helping hand. I'm nice like that...

Section 3 — Analysing Data

Q2 Fritz did an experiment to investigate the effect of air resistance on how long it takes a parachute to fall from a height. He hypothesised that:
'Increasing the surface area of the parachute will increase the time taken to fall'.

PHYSICS

His method was as follows:

- Make a parachute by cutting out a square of polythene.
- Tie a piece of string to each corner of the square.
- Tie the strings to a 5 g weight.
- Make two more parachutes of different sizes using the same method.
- Drop each parachute from 2 metres above the ground.
- Time how long it takes the weight to reach the ground.
- Repeat three times for each parachute.

His results are in the table below:

Parachute area (cm^2)	Time taken to fall (s)			
	1	2	3	Average
25	1.39	1.34	1.38	1.37
36	1.43	1.41	1.42	1.42
49	1.47	1.15	1.49	1.48

a) Write a conclusion for this experiment.

b) Write an evaluation for this experiment.

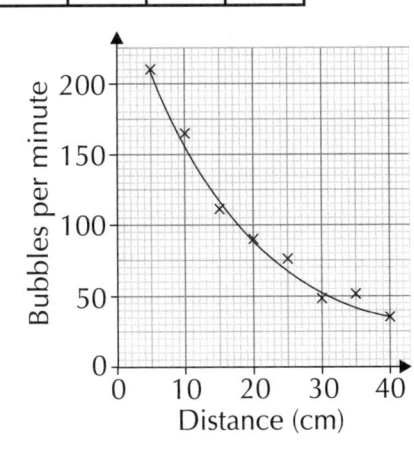

Q3 Some students are looking at the effect of light on photosynthesis. They hypothesised that 'increasing the intensity of light will increase the rate of photosynthesis'. They decided to use the amount of oxygen produced over time as a measurement of the rate of photosynthesis.

BIOLOGY

Their method was as follows:

- Fill a beaker with water and add a shoot of pondweed.
- Position a lamp 5 cm away from the beaker.
- Count the number of bubbles the pondweed produces in one minute.
- Repeat the experiment with the lamp at increasing distances from the beaker.
- Use a fresh piece of pondweed for each experiment.

The table and graph below show the results for this experiment.

Distance of lamp (cm)	5	10	15	20	25	30	35	40
Bubbles per minute	210	165	113	90	76	49	52	35

a) Write a conclusion for this experiment.

b) Write an evaluation for this experiment.

Section 3 — Analysing Data

Q4 Amy was looking at how the length of a wire affects its resistance in an electric circuit. Her hypothesis was 'increasing the length of a wire increases its resistance'.

PHYSICS

Her method was as follows:
- Set up a circuit with a battery pack, a voltmeter and an ammeter.
- Cut a piece of copper wire 5 cm long.
- Add the copper wire into the circuit.
- Record the voltage.
- Record the current.
- Calculate the resistance of the wire using your readings.
- Repeat the experiment using different lengths of wire.

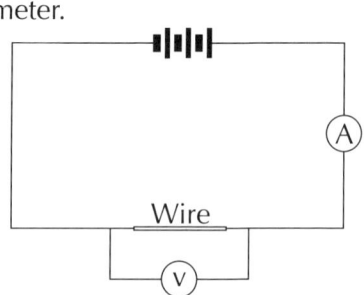

Her results are shown in the table on the right.

a) Write a conclusion for this experiment.
b) Write an evaluation for this experiment.

Length of wire (cm)	Resistance (Ω)
5	1.15
10	2.67
15	4.5
20	6.1
25	7.72
30	9.06

Q5 Some students did an experiment to investigate the effect of temperature on the rate of reaction. Their hypothesis was 'increasing the temperature increases the rate of reaction'.

CHEMISTRY

Their method was as follows:
- Measure 50 cm³ of 1 mol/dm³ nitric acid and pour it into a conical flask.
- Add zinc carbonate to the flask and put a bung in the top.
- Use a gas syringe to measure the amount of gas produced every 2 minutes.
- Repeat the experiment using a 35 °C water bath.

The table and graph below show the results for this experiment.

Time (min)	Volume of CO_2 produced	
	Room temperature	35 °C
0	0	0
2	12	20
4	22	30
6	28	34
8	32	35
10	34	36
12	35	36
14	36	36

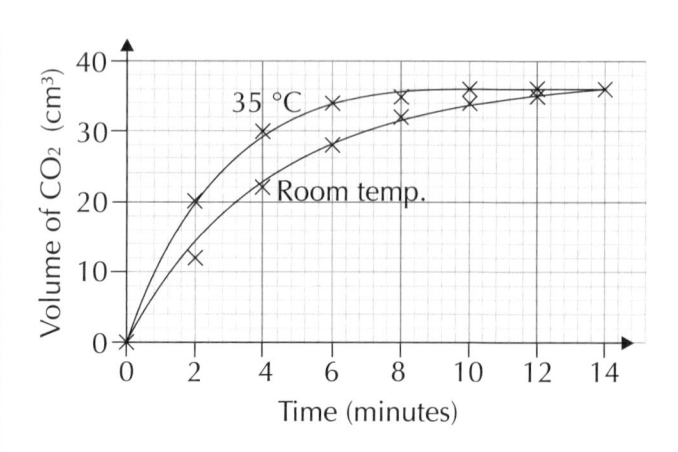

a) Write a conclusion for this experiment.
b) Write an evaluation for this experiment.

Glossary

acceleration	How quickly an object's velocity is increasing.
anomalous result	A result that doesn't fit in with the rest of the results.
bar chart	A type of graph where the height of a bar represents a quantity.
conclusion	A summary of what you've found after analysing your data.
correlation	A relationship between two things (or a measure of how closely they're related).
deceleration	How quickly an object's velocity is decreasing.
dependent variable	The thing that's measured in an experiment.
directly proportional	A relationship between two things where they both increase or decrease at the same rate.
evaluation	Where you say how well your investigation went, whether there were any problems and how you'd improve it.
gradient	The slope of a graph.
histogram	A graph where the area of a bar represents a quantity.
hypothesis	A statement that says how two or more things could be linked. It is tested in an investigation.
independent variable	The thing you change in an experiment.
indirectly proportional	A relationship between two things where one increases and the other decreases at the same rate. It can also be called inversely proportional.
line graph	A graph where straight lines show the pattern of the plotted points.
line of best fit	A line on a graph which passes though or as near to as many points as possible.
mean	The average of a set of results. It is calculated by adding together the results and then dividing by the total number of results.
negative correlation	A relationship where as one thing increases, the other thing decreases.
origin	The point on a graph where the both the x and y value are 0. It is written as (0,0).
pie chart	A round chart that is divided into sectors. The size of each sector shows the relative size of a quantity.
positive correlation	A relationship where as one thing increases, so does the other.

Glossary and Index

range How spread out a set of results is.
It is calculated by subtracting the smallest result from the largest result.

scatter graph A graph where the data is plotted as points. If a correlation is seen, a line of best fit can be drawn to show the relationship between the two variables.

significant figures (s.f.) The digits in a number (in order, starting from the first non-zero digit).

velocity How fast an object is travelling (its speed) in a specific direction.

Index

A
acceleration (calculating) 52
anomalous results 2, 21, 57

B
bar charts
  drawing 12-13
  interpreting 34-35

C
categoric data 12
conclusions 56
controls 57
correlation 42
cows 13

D
distance (calculating) 54
distance-time graphs 50

E
evaluations 57

F
formulas
  rearranging 8
  substituting into 6
frequency density 28-29

G
gradients 50, 52

H
histograms
  drawing 28-29
  interpreting 48
hypotheses 56

L
line graphs
  drawing 16-17
  interpreting 38-39
lines of best fit 21, 42

M
mean 2

N
negative correlation 42

P
percentage change 4
percentages 4
pie charts
  drawing 24-25
  interpreting 46
positive correlation 42
proportional relationships 43

R
range 2
recipe for cake 6
rounding numbers 2

S
scatter graphs
  drawing 20-21
  interpreting 42-43
significant figures 2
speed (calculating) 50

T
tables
  drawing 10
  interpreting 32

V
variables 12
velocity-time graphs 52, 54

X
x-axis 12

Y
y-axis 12